Writing Freelance

Writing Freelance

Christine Adamec

Self-Counsel Press
(a division of)
International Self-Counsel Press Ltd.

Self-Counsel Press acknowledges the financial support of the Government of Canada through the Book Publishing Industry Development Program (BPIDP) for our publishing activities.

Printed in Canada.

First edition: 2000

Cataloging in Publication Data
Adamec, Christine A., 1949-
    Writing freelance

    (Self-counsel writing series)
    ISBN 1-55180-289-9

    1. Freelance journalism. 2. Authorship—Marketing. I. Title. II. Series.
    PN153.A33 2000   808'.02   C00-910143-8

Self-Counsel Press
(a division of)
International Self-Counsel Press Ltd.

1704 N. State Street	1481 Charlotte Road
Bellingham, WA 98225	North Vancouver, BC V7J 1H1
USA	Canada

Acknowledgments

Thank you to my husband, John Adamec, for his continued assistance and moral support. Thanks also to my son Brian Adamec for his review of my chapter on the Internet and for his averting panic by quickly resolving the problem when my computer behaves inexplicably.

Contents

Samples

Worksheets

Checklist

Introduction

Are you a person with interesting ideas and an intense curiosity about a subject or many different subjects? Have you pushed this side of yourself back into the shadows of your life because you equated writing with poverty?

Let that person out. If you want to launch a writing career and at the same time make some money, the good news is that these are not mutually exclusive goals, despite what you may have heard. There are plenty of opportunities today for writers, particularly in the nonfiction field, to exercise their creative talents and bring home some bucks.

Of course you will need to do some careful planning and learn how to improve and use your skills and abilities effectively. A successful writing career doesn't just happen — so if you are a fatalistic kind of person who hopes for good karma to drop in your lap, think again about being a writer.

My purpose in writing this book is to get you started with the basics and to give you some insider information that you won't read anywhere else.

Forget everything you've heard or read about the heavy competition, the difficulty obtaining assignments, and the paltry fees that writers routinely receive. With effective marketing and basic business practices — which I'll discuss — you can and will earn good fees for your work.

Why? Because there are many editors, publishers, organizations, and individuals who need good writers. Sometimes they *desperately* need good writers. For this reason, you won't have to starve in a garret or become a stereotypical avant garde bohemian — unless you want to.

You don't have to become some kind of horrid, greedy person either. I like to say that my goal is to "do good and do well," meaning accomplish positive goals and receive adequate compensation.

What kind of people are writers? Anyone! Writers come from both poor and affluent backgrounds. Their ages range from twenty-something to retirement (some are teenagers!). The common denominator among writers who satisfy their clients and make money is that they have an urgently needed skill, for which people will pay real money.

What's it like to be a writer? The life of the successful freelance writer can be thrilling and fulfilling, but it is also hard work. Sometimes you can get so involved in a project that you lose track of time and may even forget to eat. You immerse yourself in this job.

More often, however, you'll need to jump-start yourself, particularly on those days when you'd rather clean out the cat litter than sit down and write that first draft. But the good writer writes the draft. (And cleans the litter later!)

A writing career also entails some sacrifices, and I will discuss the advantages and disadvantages of a writing business and the nuts-and-bolts issues of running a successful business. It is important to know that the writing field is not necessarily easy and, frankly, it is not always fun. But it can be a great life and provide you with a good living if you manage it properly.

So let that writer inside come on out! No matter what people have told you, the reality is that most of you can be successful writers. It's a dream that is neither impossible nor futile. I'm here to awaken that "inner writer" and start you on the path to success.

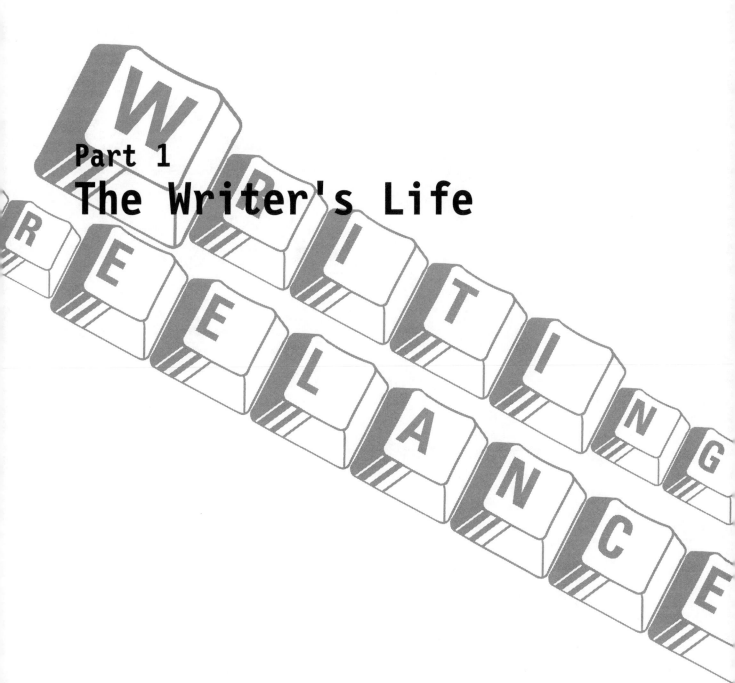

Part 1
The Writer's Life

CHAPTER 1

Is Writing For You? The Writer's Life

A writing career is both more and less glamorous than the average person realizes. It is *more* glamorous because you may have the opportunity to meet important and influential people and ask them questions that their friends and colleagues would never dare ask. It is also *less* glamorous because writing involves planning and hard work. If you've got a deadline to meet tomorrow, you may still be up at 2:00 a.m. while everyone else in your family is enjoying a deep sleep. The glamor isn't there at those times — only the hard work.

How do you picture the everyday life of a freelance writer? Many people have a stereotypical view of what it's like to be a successful writer, something like the following.

You begin your day in a leisurely way, rolling out of bed at noon, yawning, after being at a chic party the night before. After sorting through the many checks that have arrived in the mail, you consider whether to turn on the computer or take a "mental health" day. Before you can decide, your agent calls to report excitedly that 12 publishers are fighting over your latest book proposal. You yawn again. So what else is new? Then the publisher of your most recent book calls to ask if you can do a big book tour, hitting at least ten major cities nationwide. You say you'll think about it and get back to her.

The next call is from the editor of a big women's magazine, who pleads with you — please, oh please! — to write a short article based on the extensive knowledge you revealed in your new book. Oprah's producer is your next breathless caller. Can she book you for next week? Oh where is your appointment calendar? Or better, where is your secretary? Let her figure out this scheduling stuff.

If this is how you imagine the life of a freelance writer, you are in for a rude awakening. On the other hand, if you can accept that there's plenty of hard work involved and there will be a certain time when you will be learning the ropes and probably not earning much, then you may be able to make a living as a freelance writer.

It's also important to accept up front that a freelance writing career isn't just a career. It's a business; you won't succeed unless you're prepared to treat it like one. If you're a flexible and curious person, as well as one who takes your work seriously, then a career as an entrepreneurial writer may be just right for you.

> Freelance writers are their own bosses and they can turn down projects, enter new fields, and meet fascinating people in person or by telephone. Being a freelance writer is (almost) never boring.

1. Why do you want to become a freelance writer?

Before plunging into the field of freelance writing, you need to look at both the positive aspects and the possible trade-offs you may make in terms of income, time, and security. You also need to be sure you're considering writing as a career for the right reasons. Take the self-test in Worksheet 1 and then evaluate your answers based on the information below.

1.1 Let me outta here! Freelance writing has got to be better than this

Did you say that Statement 1 was "true"? Sometimes people want to escape the unpleasant environment that they're in now, so they rush off to an altogether different career. It's a better idea, however, to do some

Self-Test: Why Do You Want To Become a Freelance Writer?

Read each of the following statements and decide if it accurately describes your feelings. Circle "True" or "False," depending on your answer. Don't think about what is the "right" answer; instead select your immediate response.

1. The main reason I want to be a writer is to get away from my awful boss.	True	False
2. I think it would be glamorous to be a writer.	True	False
3. I like planning my own schedule and I'm good at it.	True	False
4. I want to be famous.	True	False
5. I want to be rich.	True	False
6. Writing is my best skill.	True	False
7. My mother thinks I'd make a great writer.	True	False
8. I have special knowledge or expertise.	True	False
9. I hate getting dressed up for work.	True	False
10. I want a challenging career.	True	False

investigation about the career you are thinking about jumping into before you make such a commitment. Freelance writing can be difficult, and you will need to be a tough taskmaster for yourself. You'll need to meet deadlines, try to please editors, and sometimes work long hours. Could you be a tough enough boss? And could you live with yourself as the boss?

1.2 Not for glamor queens or kings

As for the glamor, I think we've already exploded that myth of tinkling laughter and glittery people. It can happen, of course, but it's certainly not the day-to-day life of the freelance writer. If you want glamor, another career field would be a better one.

1.3 Declaring your independence

If you said "true" for Statement 3 because you are an independent sort of person who likes to make your own way, freelance writing may be the right field for you. You'll deal with a wide variety of people and control your workload and your time.

1.4 Fame! I want to live forever...

Statement 4 is about fame, and, unfortunately, fame is guaranteed to no freelancer. Many writers make a good living, but nobody recognizes or remembers their names. If you expect to turn heads when you enter a restaurant, don't choose freelance writing as your career. Of course, if you become a bestselling author, your chances are much improved!

1.5 Money, money, money

Was Statement 5 true for your? If you aspire to great wealth, and if this is your primary motivation in life, please don't become a writer. You should be able to make a profitable living, but it is also important to

Most small-business people don't expect to break even (i.e., have their earnings equal or exceed their expenses) during their first year of operation, and sometimes longer, because they anticipate that they will need to learn the business, create new contacts, and build up their client base. So you should plan to have sufficient funds to fall back on when you start your new career as a writer.

keep in mind that the six- or seven-figure book advances are very few and far between. That is why they make the big headlines in *Publisher's Weekly*, a trade magazine for the book industry.

1.6 Let me entertain you

If you've always loved writing and won praise for your work from teachers, bosses, and others outside your family (sorry, what your parents think doesn't count!), this is a positive indicator.

1.7 Your mother is *supposed* to love her baby girl/boy

Which leads me to Statement 7. Even if your mother is a talented writer, mothers (or fathers) are generally not good judges of the writing talents of their offspring. Positive feedback is more meaningful if it comes from someone who won't care if you're mad at him or her and doesn't have to worry about being invited over for Christmas or Hanukkah.

1.8 Having secret knowledge

Special expertise, mentioned in Statement 8, may be helpful. If you are knowledgeable about cars or boats, for example, you may be able to launch your career by writing articles or books about these topics.

However, possessing special information is not necessary. If you are able to do good research, conduct good interviews (topics covered in later chapters in this book), and then synthesize the material you've amassed into a form that captivates your readers, then these techniques may make you as successful a writer as someone with special expertise.

1.9 Goodbye neckties or pantyhose, hello jeans and T-shirts

What about Statement 9, the one that asks you if you hate getting dressed up? This is a trick question. Many writers I've talked to have told me that they loathe wearing business clothes, wriggling into pantyhose (if they are women), or wearing a tie (if they're men). As a result, most freelancers love the freedom of being able to wear jeans or shorts or whatever casual clothes they prefer. Of course, when we go out to interview someone, the business clothes need to go on.

1.10 Get that adrenaline pumping

If you said Statement 10 was true, then freelancing can be as challenging as you want it to be. You can find yourself juggling several assignments at once and interviewing five different people in one day (on the telephone), then rushing to meet that dread deadline. If you want less challenge, you cut back and take on less work. Of course, then you receive less money, unless you've worked it out that the few jobs you take all pay well.

Don't make the mistake of confusing challenge with glamor. Not that I know too much about glamor, since I haven't experienced it. But I have faced many challenges in my writing career, and you can really get the blood flowing when you have to achieve difficult assignments within impossible time frames.

2. Advantages of life as a freelance writer

There are many advantages to being a freelance writer. I discussed some of them above, but there are a few that may surprise you. (I'll get into disadvantages later on.)

2.1 You're the boss

Being in charge is a major plus for many freelance writers. You are the captain of your career and you decide what to write about. By contrast, as a staff writer you might work in an office with a boss who treats you miserably and tells you to write about things that don't interest you in the slightest. In that case, you have to grit your teeth, bear it, and soldier on in order to receive that biweekly paycheck.

As a freelance writer, you can choose never (or almost never) to deal with an unreasonable person again. If you find a wonderful editor, you can develop a working relationship with that person that could last for months or even years. You decide who to work with, who is good, and who is bad. You're the boss.

2.2 You set your own schedule

As long as you meet your deadlines, you set your own schedule. (Start missing deadlines and your career will head south fast.) You are not constrained to work between 9:00 a.m. and 5:00 p.m., and you do not have to adapt to the norm. This is wonderful news for those of us who are naturally nocturnal — if you want to finish a chapter at the crack of dawn, you can.

2.3 It's often (but not always) fun

Your title of "freelance writer" or "journalist" or "entrepreneurial writer" or "contract writer" or "galactic overlord of words" — or whatever other title you prefer — can gain you entry into many places the public never sees and open up offers the average person will never receive. You may be granted behind-the-scenes access to people and businesses other people cannot meet or know firsthand. You become the eyes and ears for your readers.

In the morning you may be interviewing a specialist in rare diseases and in the afternoon you could be talking to a trade show director.

You may be able to travel extensively and make money by writing about the cruise you just took or the whitewater rafting adventure you plan to experience.

You can be an armchair writer and interview people all over the world by telephone or even by e-mail, as I often do, asking them questions for a book, article, or report. (See chapter 11 for more about interviewing.)

2.4 You get paid for your work...and you get lots of mail

Since I was about nine years old, I have loved receiving mail. Now that I am an adult who receives quite a lot of mail in my oversized mailbox, guess what? I still love it. Okay, maybe not the bills so much. But nothing beats the treasure trove of information that arrives periodically.

Nothing, that is, but the checks that arrive in the mail. How much money can you make? It is really up to you and depends on several key factors: the type of writing you do, your contacts, how prolific you are, and the contracts you sign and sometimes create yourself.

You should not work for free unless you can identify a strong reason for doing so. For example, if you've just written a detailed book on anorexia nervosa, you may wish to promote your book by writing free or low-paying articles on anorexia for prestigious publications that could lead to increased sales of your book.

In most cases, however, it is more important that you are well paid for your hard work. (See chapter 15 for more about estimating what you should be paid.)

2.5 You save on expenses and reduce stress

When you are a freelance writer, you no longer need to rush around frantically in the morning to get ready for work and then drive in bumper-to-bumper traffic to your office in the city. Think of all the time and stress you can avoid. Your blood pressure might even go down.

You'll also save on the wear and tear on your car, and on all the gas, oil, and other expenses related to daily commutes. Of course, freelance writers do need to travel sometimes, but you can request that travel expenses be added to your fee.

You will probably save on your clothing budget, too. Many writers can wear whatever they want. If you're interviewing someone on the telephone or typing up a manuscript, it doesn't matter if you have on a flannel nightgown or a T-shirt and shorts. Or you could work stark naked. (Most of us wear clothes.) Dress up or dress down; it's your choice.

Of course, when you go out to interview someone in person, you must dress professionally in appropriate business attire. Your aim is to be taken seriously.

Some people believe that writers and others who work at home cannot be productive if they're wearing their "play clothes." They recommend that you dress for business, even if you don't go out to an office to work. If you can't produce without business clothes on, go ahead and wear them.

2.6 You can pay more attention to your family

If family members are ill, you can stay home and look after them or take them to the doctor. No frantic negotiations with your boss, no worries about whether you have enough vacation set aside or if taking the

When my first book (a how-to book on adoption) was published, I wrote articles for free for a national adoptive parents' magazine, promoting my book and gaining strong name recognition for my writing.

day off will hurt your prospects for promotion. Rearranging your schedule is usually not a problem, though if you have an interview set up that you cannot change, you'll have to work around it.

The opportunity to attend to your family's needs when necessary is an advantage. Now you don't have to put up with snide remarks about being on the "Mommy (or Daddy) track" if you need to look after your children. This doesn't mean, however, that you don't need dedicated time for work. Each writer must find a way to devote a certain amount of time to work only.

2.7 You gain recognition

All writers are thrilled when their very first article or book is published. Your name is right there for all to see! (And with luck it is spelled correctly.) You'll want to save it forever, frame it, show it to the whole world. Although it's not quite so dramatic the 200th or 500th time, it's always a rush to see your name in print.

Readers can also be appreciative. They read your article or your book and something clicks. They try what you advise and it works. Sometimes writers receive fan letters thanking them for their help in resolving a particular problem. It is tremendously gratifying to receive such letters.

If you write a book, someone somewhere will probably review it. A favorable review can be a heady experience. Good reviews will sell more copies of your book. You can also use them as stepping-stones to your next book contract.

Writers are often invited to talk about their book on the radio or appear on television. These are more opportunities to let people know about your ideas and expertise.

2.8 Sometimes (but not always) success comes fast

Although it's possible that you may have to "suffer in the trenches" for a few years before you obtain good assignments, it is also possible that they may come faster than you'd expect. The fifth or sixth magazine article I ever wrote was for *McCall's* magazine. One of my online buddies, R.G. Schmidt, a newspaper columnist and author of *Good Luck and Tight*

Sick kids? Bad weather? Not a problem. Generally, face-to-face interviews can be either rescheduled or conducted by telephone, fax, or e-mail instead.

Lines — about inshore Florida fishing (Gulf Press, 1996) — reports that he sold his first article to a major magazine, and his newspaper columns quickly developed a following.

If he or I have a "secret," I think it was that we weren't afraid to query major markets. Of course, you must expect rejections. But starting at the bottom is not necessary when you have a good idea that you think would work for a major publication.

When I asked what level of publication he targeted in the beginning of his career, Schmidt said, "The top. I have always sent my material to the best-paying market in a given genre, despite the frequently seen advice to get some bylines first. I work my way from the top down." I heartily endorse his words.

2.9 You create your own work environment

You're usually not allowed to choose your coworkers in an office environment; someone else calls the shots. Coworkers — or your boss — can sometimes be annoying and intrusive, the old, cheap, rigid chair gives you a backache, and the computer equipment at work may not be as good as the setup you have at home.

When you work for yourself, you decide how your office should look. You can have a room set aside for your work or you can use part of a room. Do you like plants hanging everywhere and scads of photos of your kids? Great. Do you do your best work while listening to rock or country music? No problem. You won't have to worry about your office cubicle neighbors anymore.

Choose the computer and office equipment that best suit your own needs, and buy an ergonomically correct chair that won't hurt your back.

2.10 You can be creative

Writers seek out information and analyze and interpret it in an intriguing way that captures readers' attention. Writers come up with new ideas and angles for stories and present them in unique, memorable ways.

When your mind is buzzing with thoughts about new ways to communicate your ideas, you can experience a heady creative experience.

2.11 Writers can change lives

Always think about your readers. Maybe your profile of an elderly woman who returned to college to get her degree will inspire a middle-aged reader to feel that it is not too late to go back to school.

Words are very powerful. The children's nursery rhyme "Sticks and stones can break my bones, but words can never hurt me" has always puzzled me. Words can destroy. More importantly (to me), words can empower.

I asked several successful writers this question: What do you think is the biggest mistake that new writers make?

Jacquelyn Lynn (a freelance business writer and columnist for *Entrepreneur* magazine):

New writers often have trouble understanding that what they're doing is a product and that it's important to give the customer what he or she wants. For example, when an editor asks for 1,500 words written at an eighth-grade reading level, that's what you should write — not 4,000 words written at a graduate school level.

Susannah Nesmith (a writer reporting on the Balkans for a variety of newspapers):

Not marketing their work to a number of different publications. Or marketing the same idea to a number of different publications without bothering to tailor the pitch to each publication.

> 📖 **Marilyn Pribus** (a writer with more than 700 sales of nonfiction and fiction to magazines and newspapers nationwide):
>
> Getting discouraged after a few rejections. The first story I tried to sell wasn't accepted until the ninth submission. Since then I've resold it nearly 30 times.
>
> 📖 **Gini Graham Scott** (author of *Work With Me! Resolving Everyday Conflict at Work* [Davies-Black, 2000]):
>
> Being afraid that someone will take their idea if they talk about it, not realizing that ideas are the easy part, and many people come up with the same idea. The key is how you can express that — and besides, ideas can't be protected legally anyway.

3. Disadvantages to the writing life

Nearly every profession has a downside. For freelance writing, many of the negative aspects are a flip side or a subset of the very advantages I've listed above! For example, you are in charge of your own work, but this means that the person who must ensure that you obtain assignments and meet deadlines, and who must keep on your case — is YOU! If you are undisciplined in your personal life and generally rely on others to tell you when and what to do, think hard before becoming a freelancer.

3.1 You must take full responsibility for your work

The inverse side to the nice feeling of being in control of your life is you must also take full responsibility. There's nowhere to hide in the hierarchy because it's just you. You must seek out work; you must fulfill your obligations.

Many freelance writers have a considerable amount of trouble pacing themselves. It may seem that you have either not enough work or far too much. If you don't have enough work, there's no boss to blame. If you have too much work to do, well, whose fault is that? The guilty party is you.

3.2 Planning your time is very important

Most freelance writers must consider not only what is due today or this week, but must also think about projects due next month or even three to six months from now. This requires careful planning — and the realization that sometimes circumstances destroy the time map you've created for yourself. A client may take a long time to get back to you on a job; another client may ask for some extra work and you feel that it would be impolitic to say no. All sorts of things can intervene in the real world.

You also need to be somewhat flexible. For example, in order to meet a particular deadline, you may need to talk to President Big from the XYZ Corporation within the next few weeks. This means that you must also take President Big's time into account. Meeting your deadline may depend on whether President Big can fit you into his or her very busy work schedule.

If you're the kind of person who wrote all your term papers the night before they were due, you must break this habit immediately. Sometimes research can take weeks or months to do; it isn't always easy. When problems crop up, you will want to be working within a reasonable time frame so you have a chance to resolve them.

3.3 Sometimes it's not fun

Most of the time it *is* fun to be a freelance writer. But I admit, sometimes I'd rather be flipping burgers...which is true of most jobs.

Sometimes you may think "Why am I doing this?" You may even ask yourself if it would not be better to get a "real job," whatever that is.

Sometimes you may not feel up to doing the work that needs to be done and done now. For example, let's say you have a cold and don't feel like interviewing the important person who has deigned to speak with you. Too bad. You talk to him now or you'll never get him at all. If you worked for the XYZ Corporation, you could call in sick. Not if you're a freelancer on deadline. So you do it. First, you give yourself a strong pep talk about how much you really want to do it. Then you put on your best "smiley face" voice and do the interview.

Other aspects of writing can be annoying or aggravating. For me, writing first drafts has always been torture. It's no fun at all. But once I have something typed into my computer, even if it's gobbledygook, most of the time I can fix it.

Other writers loathe editing their own work. They find it painful to take out their wonderful quotations or descriptions that unsympathetic editors want to delete. A good writer grits his or her teeth and tries to please the customer, and if that means taking out what the editor considers extraneous, it gets taken out.

3.4 Earnings are generally sporadic — even when you are successful

Freelance writers rarely, if ever, receive a weekly or biweekly paycheck. Instead, the checks come when they are due according to the contracts you've worked out. (And sometimes they *don't* come when they are due, an issue addressed in chapter 15.)

Be sure to track your expected income and outflow. Don't rush out and spend a big fat check if you're going to need money later on. (It is hard not to do this, but it is very necessary.)

I have received a check for $9,000 one day and then nothing for eight weeks. One's instant urge is to splurge, but resist that impulse. (Though an occasional night out is usually okay.) You need to try to plan so that your cash flow is as steady as you can make it. You should also remember to allocate some amount of money to cover your overhead over the lean periods and make a profit as well.

3.5 No company benefits

Unlike full-time employees working for others, self-employed business-people don't receive a paid vacation, paid sick time, and other benefits. If you don't work, you don't get paid. If you want to take a vacation for several weeks, you need to budget your time and money carefully. If you live in the United States and you need health insurance, you'll have to buy it yourself unless you're covered by your spouse's job. (Some writers groups offer group health insurance. See the Appendix for a list of groups.)

3.6 You must negotiate contracts and fees

One of the reasons I like having an agent is that *he* has to negotiate difficult contracts and clauses for my book contracts. However, there are still plenty of times when I must handle the negotiation myself. Keep in mind that this is a business and you should use or develop business skills. Many people dislike talking about money and negotiating contracts, but freelance writers must do this. It may not be genteel or fun, but your earnings are what you make them. Remember, writers provide a service, just like printers, publishers, lawyers, and other professionals. Never forget this.

3.7 Record-keeping can be tiresome

Writers need to track their expenses as well as their revenues. Record-keeping can be tedious but it is also essential. For example, if an editor has agreed to cover your expenses for the magazine piece (and you did *ask*, didn't you?), how will you know what to charge unless you track who you called and when, as well as, most importantly, how much it cost? You'll need to develop your own system for recording your expenses, and you'll also need to save your receipts to create an itemized bill, because editors and other clients usually want proof that you really spent X dollars and Y cents.

You also should track expenses for your own good. If you don't know where your money is going, how can you make adjustments? How can you learn from your mistakes?

Some people expect you to work for free up front, promising to share all the profits when, for example, their book is published. I've received or read hundreds of these offers. Usually they sound something like this: "I need a writer who can help me put to paper my tragic story, which millions of people will want to read. I'm sure it will be made into a made-for-TV movie as well. I can't afford to hire someone, but we can share in the profits." Usually the tragic story is that they were abused or financially ripped off and millions of people will *not* read about it — unless it is written by a professional writer who has targeted a particular group of readers.

For example, you may look at what you've spent on paper over the course of three months and discover that you've been buying paper on an as-needed basis, every few weeks whenever you run out. You might decide it would make more sense to buy your paper in larger quantities so you can get a better price. Cutting expenses is a good way to improve your "bottom line." (See chapter 16 for more on record-keeping.)

3.8 People may expect you to work for free

Too often, people expect writers to write for free. There are two reasons for this.

One reason is that they don't understand what a writer's time is worth, so they expect writers to work on projects for very low fees or for no pay. It's one thing if the writer wants to work on the project for a charitable reason, to advance his or her career, or for some other purpose. It's another thing altogether when people assume you have all the time in the world and should devote at least some of it to their writing project.

The other reason is that people assume anybody can be a writer. This means they don't think the skill is worth paying for.

Jacquelyn Lynn, who is a freelance business writer, told me about a man she had interviewed who contacted her and offered to buy her lunch in exchange for her critiquing his book manuscript. "I don't work for food," quipped Lynn, alluding to people in large cities who stand on street corners with signs saying "Will work for food." She added, "I don't mind helping people, but I'm amazed when someone wants me to do something as significant as reading and critiquing a book manuscript for free."

3.9 Marketing is a necessity

Marketing refers to the selling of both your ideas and of yourself as the best purveyor of those ideas. Most writers need to spend time marketing themselves to clients each month in order to identify new jobs. But sometimes writers can be their own worst enemies.

For example, too many writers — particularly new freelancers — are incredibly modest about their talents and are far too reluctant to broadcast their skills. Although you do not need to convince every editor that you are the greatest human who ever lived, you should be able to convey the idea that you are a talented and creative person who can do the job and can do it well. Extreme modesty is no virtue in a freelance writer. In fact, you must work against it. (Read chapter 2 on the writer's mindset!)

3.10 Rejections happen

Nobody likes it, but can you *tolerate* rejection? I contend that writers must cultivate the armor of an armadillo, because rejections come with the territory. When someone rejects your work, you must keep in mind that it is usually not personal and is certainly not a personal renouncement of you as a human.

Why do writers receive rejections? Here are some reasons:

- It was the wrong market. You queried a women's magazine about the glories of guns. Think again!

- Your query wasn't well thought out. The idea may have sounded good but you weren't quite convincing enough.

- They just ran a similar article and it's too soon for another.

- The editor had a fight with her husband and is mad at the world. (I didn't say all reasons for rejection were rational!)

There are many other possible reasons for rejections. The only common denominator is that all writers, no matter how experienced, must face rejection sometimes. A successful freelance writer does not need constant pats on the back and can take the rejections that come. They hurt briefly, they are disappointing, and they're also inevitable. You have to realize that a percentage of your queries — and of your work — will be accepted, and as you gain experience, that percentage will increase.

What do you do when your idea is rejected? You think about it and then, if you still like the idea, you try again. I've had a book proposal rejected 14 times before a good publisher purchased it. You only need one publisher. But sometimes ideas don't sell. Or you may find that a project needs to be set aside for awhile.

Don't get mad. Getting angry when you are rejected or when you don't receive a rapid reply from an editor or client is another waste of your valuable time.

"Some writers get out of kilter if their queries don't get answered quickly," says Dana Cassell, an experienced writer and the publisher of *Freelance Writer's Report* in North Stratford, New Hampshire. "The writers I have seen over the years who have been successful don't get upset if they don't get responses. Instead, they have a routine and they follow up after so many weeks. Successful writers look at rejections as a fact and they realize that it's a numbers game." Cassell says writers need to understand that in the business world, not everyone will want to buy. "Freelance writing is no different. But too many times, people look at the creative end of it and forget that writing is also a business."

3.11 You must set work/family boundaries

Although you can usually pay more attention to your family and friends when you become a freelance writer, the fact is that sometimes you need to concentrate completely on your work. This may be hard for people to understand at first. After all, you're at home, so you're not really doing anything important, right?

Family and friends may want to visit and chat. They may find it difficult to understand that you have a deadline to meet and must finish your article or chapter *now* to meet your schedule. (This is a common problem shared by everyone who works at home, no matter what his or her job.)

Polite but firm explanations are in order. Explain to drop-in visitors that even though you are at home, you are also at work. And it is not a cute little hobby or something to fill your time; it is your career and your vocation.

Many writers are shocked to find they must still budget time for childcare, especially for children who are infants and toddlers or preschoolers. They expect that they can look after the children while they work, but this is rarely satisfactory because infants and small children require a great deal of attention. You don't want the CEO of a large corporation to hear your child in the background saying, "I go potty now?" Charming to you, maybe, but not to everyone else.

On the other hand, sometimes clients may call you after 5:00 p.m., especially if they are in a different time zone. They'll also call during lunch, dinner, and just about any other time when your children are clamoring for attention. In that case, a client should be appropriately apologetic and understanding. You do, after all, have a life.

Balancing the demands of work and family can be particularly hard for a writer, especially one with school-age or younger children. What's the way around this? Your answering machine. The answering machine can screen your calls. If a call is important and you are at home, then you can pick up. (Do NOT let your three year old do the answering machine message. Do it yourself.)

3.12 Recognition isn't guaranteed

The level of recognition you seek may not be immediately forthcoming. It may not occur for years. Or ever! We can't all be best-selling authors. In fact, many writers make a good living writing for publications that others consider obscure or that many people have never heard of at all.

There are hundreds of magazines aimed at a particular field or area of interest, magazines that are not regularly perused by all your friends and colleagues — unless they are active in that particular field. If you write for these publications, you're not likely to have people comment that they've enjoyed, or even seen, your article.

Give yourself the positive feedback you need, because you can't always depend on kind words from editors, readers, friends or relatives, and colleagues.

A pet peeve of many writers is that people discount the difficulty of what they do. These people think that anyone can write. One professional writer was annoyed when his doctor said that he'd like to be a writer, if only he had some extra time. The writer retorted that he'd like to be a physician — if only he had some spare time. The doctor got the message: time is only one factor.

As well, sometimes editors and readers disagree with what you say. You may be asked to do a major rewrite of a piece you thought was well written, or you may get negative feedback in letters from readers. You learn to live with it and you learn from it.

3.13 It can get lonely

Probably every writer finds that the solitary nature of writing for a living can be difficult at times. True, you may be interviewing people on the telephone all day long and not have a moment to spare. But there is no office banter, no kidding around at the coffee machine, and none of the latest gossip.

One solution is to get out and meet with friends for lunch, join clubs, and remain an active person. Some writers become so obsessed about production that they run the risk of becoming recluses. This is a big mistake. Take walks, meet with friends, and periodically get away from your home office — even when deadlines loom. You will find that some time off can get those creative synapses in your brain activated, thus easing the writing process considerably.

It is important to develop a healthy and balanced mindset. Do you have the writer's mindset, or can you work toward evolving one? Many people find the writer's mindset to be a comfortable and natural fit, while others need to tailor it a little until it feels right. In the next chapter I describe the writer's mindset and discuss what it means to your success in freelance writing.

CHAPTER 2

The Writer's Mindset

Now that you have a basic idea of the lifestyle and the pros and cons of freelance writing — and you believe that you can be successful — what's next? You need to do a little self-analysis to ensure you have the traits a successful writer needs, and you need to work on areas that should be improved to give you the writer's mindset.

Start by filling out Worksheet 2. It can help you evaluate whether you have the potential to be and whether you are suited to becoming a freelance writer.

If you marked "frequently" for most of the statements, then you are on your way to success. If most of your answers are "sometimes," then you may need to consider whether you can reshape yourself. Some people can. If most of your answers are "rarely," you should seriously consider whether you truly wish to become a professional writer.

1. Essential traits for the successful writer

Do you have what it takes to be a successful freelance writer? Many people do, but it is you who must do the self-evaluation. Don't be too

Self-Evaluation

For each statement below, indicate whether it applies to you frequently, sometimes, or rarely.

	Frequently	Sometimes	Rarely
(a) I love to read.			
(b) I'm curious.			
(c) I like to ask questions.			
(d) I get my work done on time.			
(e) I like to set my own schedule.			
(f) I think fast and can improvise.			
(g) I'm a good listener: people open up to me.			
(h) I can be alone for hours.			

harsh on yourself, but also consider possible flaws that might make it hard for you to succeed. I think the following traits are the most necessary for success:

- Talent
- Tenacity
- Self-direction
- Ability to be self-critical but not self-blaming
- Some organizational skills
- Willingness to network/ask questions
- Basic computer skills
- Ability to meet deadlines

- Good listening skills
- Empathy
- Assertiveness
- Good family relationships

Let's take a look at these traits one by one.

1.1 Talent: Do you have enough?

Talent is important; you may have it, but not know it. If you've never been published before, it doesn't mean you don't have talent. It just means you've never been published before. So how do you know if you have the ability to be a writer?

(a) **Take a look at your past.** Did you receive good grades on term papers in high school or college? (This is *not* a prerequisite for success!) Did you enjoy writing? What were the achievements you were most proud of? Did they have anything to do with any or all of the elements of professional writing: library research, interviewing, analyzing material, as well as writing it up?

(b) **Also look at the present.** Do you write letters to the editors of newspapers or magazines? Do you wonder about issues that don't get mentioned in articles, and do you sometimes become annoyed because reporters leave out facts you think are important?

(c) **Do you love to read?** Most good writers are voracious readers who pick up words, phrases, and ideas from a variety of materials, often unconsciously.

Do you exhibit some or all of these qualities? If you do, you have the potential to be a good writer. But even if you've answered "yes" to all of these questions, you will still need a good dose of the following characteristic if you're going to be able to meet the deadlines, do the research, and survive the rejection and the editing that you'll face as a freelance writer.

1.2 Tenacity: You need stick-to-itiveness

Tenacity is another necessary quality for a successful writer. Profit-making writers are persistent and don't give up easily. If a writer can't

Sometimes interviewees are reluctant to share important information. The successful writer works hard to convince them that the information is needed and will be handled properly and fairly.

find needed information from one source after a few tries, he or she tries other sources. If an editor turns down a very good story idea, the persistent writer gives other editors the chance to learn about this great idea. If at first you don't succeed, persist, persist, persist.

1.3 Self-direction: You can't get there from here unless you know where "there" is

Maybe you can lead others, but can you be self-directed? Are you a task-oriented person? Although many editors offer guidelines, helpful hints, and sometimes even leads (e.g., contacts or ideas for prospective interviewees), the successful writer makes his or her own plan and researches other contacts and information when needed. Think about times in your past when a project needed to be done at work or school — did you step up to the challenge?

1.4 Ability to be self-critical, but not self-blaming

As the writer researches and drafts an article, he or she must constantly ask, "Does this ring true? Is this clear? Am I leaving out anything important?" This is not an internal harangue but rather a zeroing-in on areas that you could improve.

1.5 Some organizational ability

Can you read three or more different articles and find a common thread? Can you keep track of what you are doing and for whom? (This will probably not be a problem right away, but as you become more successful, you will need to pace yourself.)

1.6 A willingness to network

The more adept you are at obtaining contacts through contacts you've already made, and at leapfrogging (in an organized way) from one expert to another, the better you will be at obtaining assignments and at researching those assignments.

For example, each time you interview a person, you should ask if there is anyone else in the field that he or she can recommend you talk to. Be sure to ask for that person's telephone number. Most people are amazingly helpful about opening up their Rolodexes to interviewers

Writers don't have to be professional archivists, but they should have some kind of filing system — even if they are the only ones who can understand it!

and researchers. You save an incredible amount of time and energy when you are able to get contacts this way. Often personal referrals can lead you to people you'd never have found on your own.

When you find those people, tell them who recommended that you call and also ask for more contacts. If you don't know how to network with people, learn.

1.7 Basic computer skills

You do *not* need to be a computer genius in order to succeed at freelance writing. However, in my opinion, the days of the writer pecking away at a manual typewriter are over. Sure, you can still do it that way. But other writers will leave you in the dust. Here's why you need a computer and some basic computer skills — and if you don't have them, they are learnable:

- Editors nearly always want to receive copy on disks.

- Editors expect to be able to e-mail you.

- You may need to send your copy by e-mail.

- You can find many assignments over the Internet.

- An enormous quantity of information is available online.

1.8 Ability to meet deadlines

Missing deadlines is a key reason why new writers fail. They lose clients because of lateness and find it difficult to develop new ones.

If an editor or other customer is counting on your book, article, or newsletter and it is not completed in time, you won't last long with that editor. Don't give stories tantamount to "the dog ate my homework."

Sometimes you'll have a valid reason for not meeting a deadline, and in this case, you may be able to work out a solution with your client. For example, I have given an editor all my research notes when I was unable to complete an assignment due to a sudden illness in my family.

Often editors give a deadline that isn't the "real" deadline — it is a week or two before they actually need the copy. These editors have generally been burned in the past by procrastinating writers who turned in their work late or failed to turn it in at all. After working with you awhile and learning to trust that you will complete assignments on time, editors will tell you what the real "drop dead" deadline is.

1.9 Good listening skills

Do people like to talk to you? Are you sometimes surprised at how much people reveal to you? Congratulations, you are probably a very good listener. If not, don't worry. It's a learnable skill and writers have plenty of opportunities to practice.

Although you might assume, since you possess two ears and normal hearing, that you are an effective listener, most people are actually poor listeners. Scientists have proven that much of what is said to us doesn't penetrate at all because we are attending to our inner thoughts or outer distractions. We also think faster than another person can speak. What happens is we start to tune out the speaker, presuming we'll come back "on time." But sometimes we become so caught up in our own thoughts that when we do tune in to the speaker again, he or she has gone far beyond the point where we last listened.

As a result, the ineffective listener can miss valuable information. Good writers cannot afford to make this mistake too often. (See chapter 11 for more about becoming an effective listener.)

When you interview someone, your listening skills are tremendously valuable. If you are a good listener, you detect each nuance of the person's voice. You are aware when he or she hesitates. The person's body language and posture reveal his or her feelings as well and allow you to pick up the nonverbal cues that say what the person feels but has not said. The good listener pays attention to these signals and gains insight and information.

1.10 Empathy: Putting yourself in their shoes

Are you the kind of person people enjoy talking to? As an interviewer, you need to elicit information from a very wide assortment of people. Can people open up to you? You don't need to be a psychologist or social worker, but a basic liking of people is essential to a successful writing career.

1.11 Assertiveness: Stand up for yourself

A successful writer must have or develop the ability to step forward and say "I can do this job." Many of us have been trained not to blow our own horn.

It may seem both immodest and tacky, but how is anyone going to know you're available and you're good unless you say so? As a result, if you don't feel that you have the self-confidence to assert yourself, you need to cultivate it.

1.12 Good family relationships

Another aspect that is important to the success or failure of your venture is your family.

Will family members be supportive of your goals? Will they understand that just because you are home doesn't mean you can always pick up the clothes at the cleaners, do the grocery shopping, and so on? Will they understand that sometimes deadlines mean you will have to work nights, weekends, and sometimes on holidays too?

Conversely, you mustn't take advantage of your family's ability to be understanding and supportive and allow your work to spill over into most of the time you spend together.

Taking on a writing business will bring changes to your life. Changes send out ripples that affect your family. So there may be an adjustment period until your family understands the new role you have chosen.

```
Be sure to establish an office area that is not too readily available
to your spouse, friends, or children. I recommend this as a safety
measure. A friend who formerly ran a mail order business let her son
play computer games on the same computer where she had stored her
entire mailing list of 5,000 names, which, alas, she had failed to
back up. A virus on her child's game destroyed all her data and was
the beginning of the end of her business. It was not the child's
fault; I'm sure he felt terrible. But the lesson to be learned here
is to treat your own work seriously and that is one step toward having
your family treat it seriously too.
```

2. Essential qualities of the writer's mindset

Many people new to the publishing field are very timorous and shy. This is understandable. Your first day on any job — as a teacher, a lawyer, a cashier in the local supermarket — can be nerve-racking. It's no different for the new freelance writer — it can be scary at first. The problem is that many writers take far too long to get themselves into the writer's mindset.

What is this mysterious mindset? I see it as a combination of attitudes that motivate behavior and enable a writer to succeed. I think the traits you need to already have or to cultivate are the following:

- Self-acceptance

- Humility

- A businesslike attitude

- Willingness to look at the world from other perspectives

- An ability to position yourself as a solution to a problem

- An understanding of your role

- A professional attitude

2.1 Self-acceptance

Many writers experience periods of self-doubt and worry. This is normal. But you will need to overcome any overarching feelings of inferiority or anxiety that can set you back. One way to accept yourself as a competent writer is to avoid saying to yourself "I'm a writer?" with a question mark on the end. Neither should you overdramatize it with an exclamation mark. "I am a WRITER!"

Here's an easy exercise for you. I want you to practice saying "I am a writer," and make it sound convincing! Say it 12 times. Say it in your living room or in front of the bathroom mirror if you want to, but do say it. After awhile, the statement will sound more believable to you. This is a good start. You can expand on the statement, too. Say "I act the way a writer acts and I think like a writer. Therefore, I am a writer."

Some people fear saying that they're writers — even to themselves — because they haven't yet been published, or have *only* had five pieces published, or *only* one book, or have *only* written fiction or nonfiction, and so on. You are a writer if you say you are a writer. Maybe not a published writer yet, but a writer nonetheless.

Your goal, as a writer, is to be published and paid and to make a profit. As you work toward that goal, you *are* a writer.

2.2 Humility is important too

"Wait a minute," you may think. "Did she build me up only to knock me down again? What's with this "humility" angle?"

I don't think that self-acceptance and humility are mutually exclusive traits. I am referring to humility here in a special way. It is the willingness to ask questions that you think might sound "stupid" and the willingness to venture into areas where you will sometimes have to strain your brain. If you don't ask those questions, you run the very real risk of shortchanging your readers later on. And if you don't stretch yourself once in awhile, you'll eventually lead a more contracted existence. Writers need to be able to reach out self-confidently, yet with the knowledge that others often know much more than they do about many different topics.

Writers aren't expected to know everything about everything. We aren't supposed to be the world's smartest people. We are people who can learn about a topic through interviewing and research, then synthesize what we have learned and present the information in a format that works for our readers.

2.3 Businesslike attitude

A good freelance writer takes his or her work very seriously. This is, after all, a business. This means that, in most cases, you will not go out to interview anyone who catches your interest about whatever whim strikes you at the moment, assuming that you will then write an article or book that editors will clamor to publish. Such an assumption and such behavior are marks of an amateur.

Instead, the professional writer comes up with unique, marketable ideas and collects enough information to make them sound intriguing.

He or she then offers the idea to an editor or client in the form of a "query letter" or "proposal." (I discuss both queries and book proposals at much greater length in chapter 5 and chapter 7.) Then, after receiving a go-ahead from a customer, the professional writer researches and writes the piece. Act like a pro yourself by following these guidelines, and you will increase your probability of success.

2.4 A willingness to look at the world from other perspectives

Many new writers erroneously assume that if *they* are interested in a subject, the whole world will share this interest. This is just not true. We live in a diverse society, and the editors and publishers who succeed are well aware of who their readers are — how old they are, how affluent, what interests them, and much more. They want to satisfy their readers. Your job is to help the editors achieve that goal. To do so, you need to "think out of the box."

Maximize your business by finding ideas you'd like to write about, ideas you have good reasons to believe people would like to read about, and looking at them from as many different perspectives as you can come up with. Get into the habit of asking who this subject would appeal to and how to make it appeal to more people. How can this subject be intriguing to adolescents or the aged? To people fascinated by politics or by beautiful art?

Often you will find the same research can be used over and over by rethinking how it could interest a different audience of readers.

2.5 An ability to position yourself as a solution to a problem

When you are perceived as someone who has the answer to a problem, you are much more desirable to a client, whether that person is an editor, a corporate public relations person, or anyone else who hires freelance writers.

How can you position yourself as a solution? That partly depends on how well you can figure out what the client needs. If you have a new idea for a magazine, for example, your solution is to provide the editor with interesting copy that fits in well with the magazine's other material and hasn't been written to death by other writers.

Even if you have an idea that seems just right for a specific publication, an editor may know of key people that he or she would like interviewed. If you've already researched and written the article, you've done a lot of extra work for no extra pay.

If you are hired to rewrite badly written text for a publisher, you are the solution because you can improve material that the client needs. You must be able to get at least partway into the client's mindset. One way to do this is to review material published in the past and see how you could do it differently or better.

You might be a solution to someone's problem in the following situations:

- If you live in an area that interests the client and you have access to information he or she wants. I have been asked to cover medical conferences a day or two before the conference. Why? Because I have done medical writing, the conference is taking place near my home, and the client can't find anyone else to do the job.

- If you can provide copy fast. Maybe the problem is that the client needs a story and needs it right now.

- If you can capture new readers or provide intriguing information to regular readers because you are an expert in some area or have a special interest.

These are only a few examples of how you can be the answer to a client's fervent prayers for help. Several times I have called an editor with an idea I think is exciting. I have pitched myself as a writer and presented the idea, only to hear the editor say, "I don't like that idea because we already did it a few months ago. But could you write about...(fill in the blank)? We really need that!"

If you apply for a job as an employee, your skills and talents are considered as well as what the employer thinks you will be able to do for the firm over the long term, for at least months and maybe years. But when you are hired on as an entrepreneurial writer, you are needed to solve a particular problem or to do a particular job, not to perform over the next year or next few years. The client knows that he or she can hire you for this job and never use you again if you don't work out. Thus, it is how you are perceived as a solution to a problem, rather than as an ongoing asset to the business, that is important.

What do I say when that happens? "Yes!" I can always pitch the original great idea to another editor, but my job as a freelancer is to respond to the needs of my clients.

2.6 Understanding your role: Freelance writers are different from full-time employees

Being an entrepreneurial writer is very different from being an employee. This is a big attitudinal leap. Let me illustrate with an example. I was contacted by a man who asked me what a 50-year-old engineer with 30 years' experience is "worth" as a technical writer; that is, how much should he charge for his work?

He was asking the wrong question. Your level of experience is only part of the equation — it is primarily the job itself that must be evaluated, and every job is different depending on how long it is, how much research is required, how quickly it must be done, and other factors that vary greatly depending on who does the job and who assigns the job. Sometimes writers get frustrated because there are no set answers.

When you apply for a full-time job as an employee, you are the product. As a result, your academic credentials may be terribly important. Conversely, when you seek a freelance assignment, it is the job itself that is paramount. You are the means for the client to get what he or she wants and needs.

In a way, you are like the production line that will make the widgets in a factory. If you can make beautiful or practical or complicated widgets — depending on what the client thinks his or her customers will love — you should do well. The point is that you yourself are not the widget. But if you are a full-time employee, at least for the short-term, then you *are* the widget. This is a paradigm shift that you need to make when you enter the wonderful world of freelance writing.

I have seen people with Ph.D.s in English fall flat on their face in the field of freelance writing — not because they weren't gifted at writing, but because they were unskilled at the art of simple business practices and were unwilling to learn. They refused to work with customers who would not agree with their conception of a project. They saw themselves, and not the work they could create to the client's specifications and satisfaction, as the product. This is also why people with high school diplomas or college degrees in all sorts of disciplines can succeed at writing if they have the right mindset.

2.7 Present a professional attitude

Never forget that when an editor hires you for a magazine or business assignment, you are representing his or her company. Even though you are a freelancer, any people you interview for the assignment will automatically associate your attitude, appearance, and overall behavior with that publication, so be sure to be professional in every way and temporarily adopt the client as your employer.

Some editors have complained that they have been embarrassed by freelance writers they hired who showed up to interview people when dressed sloppily and who displayed a very careless attitude. Do you think they hired those writers again? Not likely.

3. Yes, you can develop the writer's mindset

If you don't think you have the traits I've discussed, and if you still want to be a writer, is it possible to develop these traits? Sure it is! Everyone isn't born confident and talented. We work toward those goals. And one way to become confident, even before you have acquired the skills of a seasoned writer, is to act like you're confident.

In an earlier part of this chapter I told you to state to yourself aloud that you are a writer. Here's another helpful exercise for a new writer: Tell at least five people that you are a writer. Not that you are "going to be" or "hope to be" or any other form of equivocation. Do not laugh or qualify the statement in any way.

Observe what reactions you get. If someone asks you if you've been published or what you are working on, you can say that you are new to the field, or you can be vague and say that you write about "a variety of topics." It doesn't really matter. The act of stating in a serious tone that you are a writer can make you feel like a writer and help you achieve that goal. One of my former writing class students did this exercise several times and then she was offered a job as a writer on a local newspaper. She had very little experience but she was smart and confident and she was also a very good writer.

The bottom line here is, get an attitude! Better yet, get a writer's attitude. It truly can mean the difference between success or failure and between earning five figures or much less.

A major misconception I hear frequently is that your pay for writing should be equivalent to how many advanced degrees you have earned and how much work experience you have gained. It usually doesn't work that way in the field of freelance writing.

The secret of success as a freelance writer can be summed up in this equation:
S=T+P+CS
Success equals Talent plus Persistence plus Customer Satisfaction.

Part 2
Who Needs Writers? Finding Clients for Your Work

CHAPTER 3

Who Hires Writers and Why?

Now that you've developed the writer's mindset and are prepared for the freelance lifestyle, you need to learn about the breadth of potential markets for your talents. Who hires freelance writers and why do they need them?

1. Writers are always in demand

There are many reasons why writers are needed and why you can succeed in the field of publishing with persistence and hard work. Sadly, it appears that fewer and fewer people learn how to write effectively in school or college. This shortfall of talent and experience has increased the demand for effective communicators because editors and business-people who hire writers must select from a diminishing pool of talent.

Here are just a few of the types of markets and writing jobs that may suit your particular skills and services (note that I discuss writing for magazines and newspapers in chapter 4 and writing books in chapter 5):

📄 Corporations and other businesses

- Trade magazines
- Consumer magazines
- Newsletters
- Technical writing
- Medical writing
- Ghostwriting
- Project fixing

1.1 Corporations and other businesses

With downsizing and layoffs in many major corporations, there are increasing opportunities for work to be contracted out to writers. By using a freelancer, the company can get a fast turnaround, pay a flat rate, and avoid extra costs for benefits (i.e., vacation time and sick time).

Corporations publish newsletters, reports, news releases, and a wide array of other communications. They may depend on writers to produce one article or sometimes all the copy for an entire newsletter. They want good writers who can produce effective material rapidly.

Many businesses and organizations need writers who can produce articles for in-house publications. They often don't advertise this need because they operate on a referral basis and call upon writers infrequently. These opportunities can become very lucrative for writers.

Associations and small businesses need writers to assist them with public relations — writing news releases, articles about their business to submit to trade publications, and business brochures and pamphlets.

Businesses use ghostwriters to prepare special reports, proposals, and articles (see section **7.** below). A ghostwriter does not receive a byline — that is, your name doesn't appear on the piece — so even though you've done the research and writing, don't expect to see your name anywhere on the final product. Why? Because you're not a "big name" nor are you on staff. The name of someone within the company may be given as the "author" of the piece or there may be no author credit at all. But your name appears in one very important place — on the check!

There are also opportunities to write for Web sites (see chapter 12 on the Internet). This is a market for writers who can "write tight" and turn around copy quickly.

Some businesses need scriptwriters for videos that may be used for training, promotion, or a wide variety of purposes. The skills needed for scriptwriting are different from those needed for magazine feature writing because writers must take into account the visual aspect. These skills can be learned, however, and this field can be very lucrative.

Contact the public relations department of a large corporation, the president or owner of a small company, or the director of an association to learn about the organization's writing needs.

I asked published writers this question: "If you could recommend that new freelance writers memorize one statement, what would it be?"

R.G. Schmidt, newspaper columnist: "Accuracy and ethics are your most important tools."

Susannah Nesmith, newspaper writer reporting on the Balkans: "Look at every story and every market in terms of its ongoing potential."

Marilyn Pribus, a writer with over 700 nationwide magazine and newspaper credits: "Your job is to make the editor's job as easy as possible."

freelance facts

1.2 Trade magazines

Trade magazines are aimed at members of a trade or profession; there are trade magazines for artists, physicians, paralegals, and many other occupations or businesses. Take a look at the current edition of *Writer's Market* to see how many trade magazines are described — and understand that this reference book only skims the surface! (See the Appendix for bibliographic information.)

Trade magazine editors are always looking for good writers. You don't need to be an artist or a physician if you have the ability to interview people and get interesting and vital information. This is a skill that can be learned, though you may need to convince the trade editor you can learn quickly and get a handle on what is needed to write about a particular field. (For more about talking to editors, see chapter 8.)

1.3 Consumer magazines

Consumer magazines — those popular magazines you see on the rack at your local newsstand — need writers too. The more well-known publications are more difficult markets to penetrate, particularly for the novice writer, but if you have a unique idea or local slant that might interest many others, then you should give them a try.

Popular consumer magazines generally pay well and pay "on acceptance," as opposed to "on publication." But don't expect to hang your whole career on writing solely for magazines with very high name recognition. Few writers concentrate all their efforts on writing for the glossy magazines. I cover magazine writing at length in chapter 4.

1.4 Newsletters

With the increasing accessibility of desktop publishing, many large and small companies, associations, nonprofit organizations, and others have launched newsletters. And newsletter editors need copy. Many of them will beg for free information. Others are willing to pay for good copy.

Newsletter publishers often like to contract out work because it is cost-effective — no benefits, no vacation pay, etc.

If writing for the newsletter is just another chore for the staff, you may be able to turn it to your advantage. Offer to write a piece "on spec" (that is, you will write a piece and the editor may or may not publish it, depending if he or she likes it.) If the editor is happy with your work, he or she may give you more assignments until you are a necessary part of the newsletter, whether the editor realizes it or not. A newsletter can represent steady income for the entrepreneurial writer who may write some or even all of the content.

Generally, newsletter articles are tightly written in a style similar to a newspaper piece. The difference is that your copy is highly targeted to the interests of the readers, whether they are adoptive parents, train collectors, physicians in a group practice, or employees of one company.

1.5 Technical writing

If you've ever tried to decipher what in the world your computer manual says, you can understand why the world needs more technical writers. You don't have to be an engineer or a "techie" to write manuals or other technical communications for companies or publishers. What you do need is the ability to learn what the readers need to know, how to ask the experts the questions and understand their answers, and how to express the information as simply and clearly as possible.

Technical writers explain how to perform a certain procedure or how to comply with new government regulations, and they do it in plain language. I have written about eye surgery (for eye surgeons), environmental surveys, funeral planning, and many other topics that are targeted to specific audiences.

Some tech writers find jobs on their own while others seek out jobs with temporary service agencies or agencies that specialize in technical writing assignments. (See the Appendix for a partial listing of such agencies.)

1.6 Medical writing

Healthcare organizations and consultants need writers, especially now. A changing healthcare field means there is a strong demand for medical/business writers. You don't have to be a doctor or nurse to interview doctors, nurses, and medical researchers about their work. Most medical experts are very pleased to share their knowledge — although pinning them down to a specific time for an interview isn't always easy.

With the aging of the population and the huge bulge of baby boomers entering middle and old age, more and more people will be seeking information on medical treatments, aging, and other topics. Who can write about these subjects? Maybe that person is you.

New technology in the health and medical sector also offers opportunities for writers. Every new development or critical issue in the health field in North America needs a writer to explain it. In some cases, the rest of the world is your readership.

Sometimes physicians themselves need writers. You don't really think doctors write their own books, do you? Not very often! Instead, in most cases, books "authored" by physicians are really written by ghostwriters or by coauthors who write the whole book. I have ghostwritten chapters and books for physicians and been well paid for such work. One caveat: physicians are often very controlling and demanding and thus can be difficult people to work with. Be sure to have a good contract and talk to the doctor a few times, preferably in person, before you agree to any project.

Health benefits firms and consultants or newsletter publishers who cover benefits issues also need medical and business writers.

1.7 Ghostwriting

Politicians, teachers, physicians, athletes, and people from all walks of life hire ghostwriters. In many cases they may be competent writers but don't have the time to research or write a piece. In other cases they are not competent writers and want to hire a writer to transform their thoughts into a coherent and interesting book or article. Many books by famous personalities are actually written by ghostwriters for hefty fees. Ghostwriters are also used by trade magazines, professional newsletters, and other publications.

Many individuals seek the services of ghostwriters because they have a unique story they cannot write effectively themselves or because they need a manuscript polished. I was hired by a woman who wanted to win the "Mother of the Year" prize offered by an organization and she needed a great resume. She hired me, I carefully crafted her resume, and she won the prize. Other clients may hire you to assist them with a book proposal or other type of proposal, or to write a book itself. I prefer to limit my work for individuals to people who are professionals (attorneys, physicians, and others), but even they can be difficult to work with.

If you decide to work on a project for one person, make sure that you are clear on the following aspects of the job:

- The primary goal of the client (e.g., to persuade readers of his or her opinion, show how smart he or she is, to sell at conferences, to educate the general public)

- When the job is due

- How many words the job should be

- What format the client wants the job in, down to details such as double-spacing

- The tone the client wants (i.e., serious, humorous, authoritative)

Thinking of being a ghostwriter?

Ask yourself these questions:

(a) Would I mind if my client acts as if he or she wrote every word — and even forgets that I did the job?

(b) Would I mind that my name would not be on this book or article that I spent a lot of time and work on? Is it important for my name to be prominent? (A ghost is invisible. If you can stand that, ghosting may work for you.)

(c) Can I stand it if the client takes a well-written piece and turns it into a mess because he or she feels it needs to be changed? (If a client is paying, he or she has the right to do this.)

(d) Can I deal with people who may be difficult and downright unreasonable? Am I assertive enough to stand up for myself? (Most ghostwriting clients are fine, but some are just horrible, and sometimes you can't tell at the beginning of the job what they'll be like.)

1.7.a Pros and cons of ghostwriting

On the plus side, there are many people who will pay writers to write for them, whether it is a personal story, family history, adventure, or other type of books or articles. The market is wide open.

On the negative side, if you ghostwrite for an individual as opposed to a company, you will usually find that your client has a strong emotional attachment to his or her story. Often the client perceives it as the achievement of his or her lifetime. As a result, your client can become unreasonable about the book, intruding on your personal life and making unrealistic demands. If your client calls you in the evenings to talk about the book, gently tell the client that this is unprofessional and insist that he or she stop. If the client demands that you find a publisher for the finished manuscript, point out that this is not part of your job (as long as you didn't agree in a contract that you would find a publisher).

Another problem with working for individuals as opposed to corporations is that individuals often plead poverty and beg you to give them the lowest rate possible. It is understandable that they should try this tactic, but don't fall for it. If a client can't afford your fees, which should be fair, based on the terms and conditions needed to complete the job, then he or she should hire someone else.

There are two things you should remember when considering a ghostwriting project:

(a) *Always get money up front.* A person isn't really serious about hiring you if he or she won't sign a contract and give you an advance payment.

(b) *Always maintain a professional distance.* Sometimes clients think that if you are smart enough to write words for them, you must also be smart enough to hear and resolve all their personal problems. This is one place where you do not want to be an effective listener. Tune it out. Pay attention to the project instead. You can be nice and yet professional.

When you ghostwrite a book, in addition to your fee, ask for a percentage of the royalties in the event that the book is sold and becomes a bestseller. The client may say no, but he or she may also say yes.

Checklist 1 is an outline of key questions you should ask yourself and your client every time you consider a ghostwriting project. Prepare your own checklist and adapt the questions to address your own concerns and needs. And be careful! I have done ghostwriting for wonderful people and a few monsters. At one point I swore I'd never work as a ghostwriter again unless my client had a complete and recent psychiatric evaluation that I could review. I have since backed away from that position, but I am still careful before agreeing to a contract.

The questions in the checklist may make ghostwriting sound like a daunting and fearsome task. While this isn't always the case, it is important to ask the tough questions right away to avoid problems later on.

Deciding To Take On a Ghostwriting Project

1. Questions to ask yourself for every ghosting job you consider:

   (a) Do I understand what this person wants and can I do it?

   (b) Do I have enough time to take on this project?

   (c) Is this job interesting and possibly even fun?

   (d) Is the client offering enough money? (Ask for more than you think you will need; you will probably be glad you did.)

2. Information to elicit from your potential client:

   (a) What is the client's true agenda in hiring me to do this work? Is it because he or she is not a good writer or lacks confidence? Or does the client not have enough time?

   (b) What hidden agendas are there? Does the client seek fame and fortune or does he or she want to right a perceived wrong?

   (c) Will the client listen to your advice? (It's often hard to get an accurate answer to this, as clients will be on their best behavior at first.) Where can you see potential problems?

   (d) What does the client expect from you? Don't assume it is merely writing the book. He or she may also want you to sell the book to an agent or publisher, do innumerable rewrites, and answer all questions and concerns that come up. How much work does he or she want from you, how much time will he or she take up, and how much are you willing to do?

   (e) Do you think you can get along with this client? No matter how many dollars he or she is waving in your face, if your gut instinct screams "No," you should listen.

1.7.b Contracts are essential

You must have a contract that clearly sets out all terms and conditions. You also need to set ground rules for your client. It's too easy to think that what the client meant was X, when maybe he or she really meant Y. Put it in writing and make sure you both agree to what's in the contract.

The most you should promise is that you will write the book or article and give one free rewrite. This prevents clients from changing their minds many times, because they know up front they can have one rewrite only. If you wish to go one step beyond and provide some assistance in marketing, be sure to add that on to the fee you've negotiated. Even if you think the story has great commercial potential, don't guarantee publication.

What if your client accepts your ghostwritten manuscript and pays you, and then an editor expresses interest in the manuscript but tells the client that more rewriting is necessary? If the client accepted your work and paid you, then your job is done. In fact, I make this statement in my contract. Later, if he or she needs more work to be done on the book, you should charge more money — assuming that you are willing to take on the task.

In most cases you should ignore anyone who tells you they have a wonderful idea that will inevitably become an instant bestseller, and that they will "split the profits with you." I don't work for free for individuals, and I advise you against it too. For more information on this topic, read chapter 5 on writing books.

Some writers say they could never ghostwrite because they must have their names on everything they write. They work for recognition as much as for money. If you can't bear the thought of not having a byline or, even worse, seeing another person's name on your words, don't be a ghostwriter.

1.8 Project fixing

Another opportunity for freelance writers is to take over projects that other writers have dropped. The original writers may have left the project because they were sick, daunted by the topic, unable to make the deadline, or for a variety of other reasons. Often editors, businesspeople, and those who hire ghostwriters need good writers as "manuscript doctors," to "fix" or rewrite manuscripts. I have taken over chapters and even entire books that were written by others and needed to be rewritten, reports that were started and dropped, and many other projects started by others.

The good news about taking over someone else's project is that the customer is often so dissatisfied with it, and so frustrated, that practically anything you do will be perceived as wonderful. The bad news is that by the time the customer finds you, he or she is often frantic to get the job done immediately and, therefore, cannot give you much time to do it.

If you find yourself in this situation, scope out the job to see what has already been done. You may be able to use some of the work the previous writer did, or you may have to scrap everything and start from scratch. Ask to see any research materials from the previous writer, if they are available, *before* you cost out the job. Also ask for as much as one third of the total fee to be paid in advance, and request telephone and fax expenses as well as travel expenses if they are needed. Write your own outline of what is needed for the project and clear it with the customer before you begin serious work.

2. Who should you write for?

In the next two chapters I look more closely at writing for magazines, newspapers, and books. This will give you an idea of the demands and possibilities of these different markets and should help you decide where to concentrate your efforts.

CHAPTER 4

Writing For Magazines and Newspapers

Many writers cut their writing teeth on magazine articles or newspaper pieces. And many find article writing so appealing that they stick with it for their entire careers. I am one person who began my career writing newspaper and magazine articles, and I have written hundreds of features on many different topics. Writing short pieces on a tight deadline is challenging and fun. In this chapter I talk about the basics you must know for success, including the major genres of writing and key tips on breaking into the world of feature writing.

1. Different genres for different folks

Almost any form of nonfiction, short or long, can be classified into a specific genre.

1.1 The personality profile (biography)

People love to read about other people, whether it is the elusive Michael Jackson or an average person who survived a difficult crisis.

The personality profile is a wonderful genre for the novice as well as the experienced freelancer. You may not realize this, but fascinating people live in your own backyard as well as thousands of miles away. The trick is to find them — and it's not that difficult. Read newspapers. Talk to people. Keep your ears and eyes open.

Sometimes the important person is thousands of miles away. I profiled the Canadian regional manager of the Toronto-based National Marine Manufacturers Association, although I live in Florida. Using my interviewing skills over the telephone, I obtained information my readers and trade show managers would love.

It's important to understand the genres of newspaper and magazine articles so that you can tailor your work to the needs and desires of the editor.

I have also interviewed many people in my own city, including an amateur radio expert who discussed an upcoming conference, a 70-year-old woman who just received her bachelor's degree in social work and is planning on becoming a social worker, and a successful insurance saleswoman who was on welfare ten years ago.

Newspapers, trade magazines, and general interest magazines are starved for good personality profiles. Their editors know that people like to read about people for inspiration. The family that tirelessly works with a disabled child inspires other families whose children suffer from similar disabilities. The woman who escaped poverty to become a wealthy salesperson probably has some good secrets and advice to share.

Personality profiles provide entertainment, information, and juicy gossip. The personality profile is frequently a favorable piece, although in some cases it is neutral or even negative.

1.2 The how-to article

The how-to piece offers practical advice to the reader on how to achieve some goal: how to program a computer, put up wallpaper, or become a writer.

In this genre, the writer needs to provide practical and often step-by-step details that a reader can follow, a kind of blueprint for success. How-to books or articles are extremely popular and there are many opportunities in this field.

Think about a skill that you and your friends or colleagues already have, or information you already know, which someone, somewhere might find valuable. My very first article back in 1981 was on how to plan a party. I hadn't planned a party in years — but my friends had, so I obtained practical and usable information from them, then wrote that article and many more for the same editor.

The book that you are reading is a how-to book, also known as self-help.

Since then I have written on how to adopt a child (newspaper and magazine articles and books), how to amuse your child when you're a noncustodial parent and the child is visiting you for the weekend (an editor thought up this topic), how to position yourself to get promoted, how to get paid if you are a physician, and many more topics.

1.3 The investigative article

In the investigative piece or exposé you describe some beliefs, statements, or actions of a person or organization and expose the flaws or wrongdoing. There are plenty of bad people, crimes, and problem areas out there to write about if taking on tough issues appeals to you, but investigative writing can be difficult and is certainly not for the faint of heart. It is very important that your information is accurate, and, whenever possible, you should obtain corroboration from at least two different sources for every important fact.

1.4 General information/educational article

Many articles or books provide general information for readers who have interest in a topic but don't want to rush out and learn everything about it. What these readers need instead is a general overview of the field. Your job is to learn as much as possible about the topic and provide your readers with the important basics that are of interest. You also often provide sidebars (information or lists that are not included in the text but are set off from the article in a box) of other sources, in case readers want to learn about this topic in more depth.

The general interest article gives the reader a taste of the subject and points in the direction of more solid information if he or she wants to pursue it.

1.5 Entertainment article

In the entertainment genre, you amuse and/or entertain your readers. Think *People* Magazine — it's just one of many examples of a successful entertainment publication. Often this genre is combined with others. For example, you may profile a public figure in an entertaining way. You may write a round-up or a personal experience piece. Often general information written in a light and easy style falls into this genre.

Readers of this type of piece want to be amused and diverted, and they don't want to do any heavy thinking, which is understandable. All writing should not be ponderous or painful.

1.6 Editorials/op-eds

In editorials pieces you take a stand on an issue and present the evidence for your view. People read editorials because they, too, have a strong position on the issue — which may or may not correspond with yours. In fact, other writers may write their own editorials to refute the points you make, and the exchange can become quite heated. On the other hand, you may be able to provide information on a problem that people don't realize is a serious one.

An editorial may be written strictly as an information piece, but often it is written as a call for action. Sometimes editorials or op-eds (so called because they appear on the page opposite the editorial page in a newspaper) are written as humorous and entertaining pieces. Pick up any newspaper and you will find editorials. Many newspapers publish guest editorials; however, they may pay very little or nothing at all for your work.

1.7 The round-up

In a round-up article you ask many people the same question and write an article summarizing the responses. Often the people who are asked the question are celebrities. They may have little or no expertise on whatever is asked, but because they are famous, what they say will interest readers.

On the other hand, sometimes the people you interview are experts. I have interviewed nursing home experts, asking about various issues or problems, for a trade magazine for nursing homes. Some round-ups include the view of the "person in the street," which means anyone the reporter gets a response from.

This genre is interesting to readers because it gives them a quick snapshot of the opinions of a group of people. Round-ups often appear in columns as well as magazine and newspaper articles.

1.8 Personal experience pieces

Personal experience pieces can be humorous little pieces or bare-your-soul articles. The common denominator of the personal experience piece is that the writer has experienced a problem or knows someone who has (for example, some authors excel at "as told to" stories, retelling the experience of someone else). Often such a piece is written to educate and help readers. There is usually an element of emotion in such pieces, possibly strong emotion depending on the issue or problem.

Personal experience pieces resonate with others who now or in the past have had the same problem as the one you are writing about. Often it is a problem within the family or a health problem, although personal experience pieces are not restricted to those categories.

1.9 Problem solver

Related to both the personal experience piece and the how-to article is what I call the professional "problem solver." You research and write about a problem faced in a field or profession and discuss how others have solved it. These articles are very much in demand and always will be. For example, you could write about how a business can get more customers, make more money, save time, and cope with competition. The problems are common to all businesses, and articles that give solutions will always interest people.

1.10 Combined genres

Many articles or books combine elements of different genres. For example, the personality profile can be a light, entertainment piece that makes its subject want to enshrine it over his or her mantel, or it may be a more balanced investigative piece that shows its subject's flaws.

2. Getting into magazines and newspapers

Okay, let's say you want to launch your freelance career by writing for magazines or newspapers. This can be a lucrative choice if you succeed. What are the basics you need to know?

2.1 Breaking into magazine writing

To start with, you need to learn how to write a query letter describing your idea. (Query letters are discussed in detail in chapter 7. See also Samples 3 and 4 in that chapter — they show two different query letters.) You want your letter to attract the attention of the magazine feature editor.

How do you know who to send the letter to? You check *Writer's Market*, *Writer's Digest*, and other writing publications and find the name of an editor. Never ever send the letter blindly to "The Editor." This is the kiss of death!

You could also check the masthead of a recent edition of the magazine you're interested in writing for. The masthead is usually near the front of the magazine and is a box that lists the editorial staff. It will also give you the correct title for each person, his or her position, and the mailing address and telephone number of the magazine.

> It may sound silly, but an editor-in-chief does not wish to be called a mere "editor," so get that title right. Also, double-check the spelling of the person's name.

2.1.a The chronology of submitting your idea

What happens after you send a query? The basic steps are:

(a) The editor replies, saying either no or yes.

(b) If the editor says no, you try somewhere else. (Assuming you're still interested in doing this piece.)

(c) If yes, you and the editor agree upon how many words you should write, when the article is due, and how much you will get paid and when.

The following are basic tips for magazine feature writing:

- Stay within the boundaries of the word count you and the editor have agreed upon. It is usually okay if the editor says a feature should be 2,000 words and your final product is 2,100, but don't submit 3,000 words. Edit it down.

- Emulate the style of the magazine. If it uses quotations, you should use them. If the magazine uses statistics, try to find some. Are the articles written in simple language or are they made up of long sentences and multisyllabic words? You don't have to take on the persona of previous writers, but the tone of your writing should complement and fit in with the magazine's style.

📃 Think about what sidebars might fit. Many magazine editors love to break up an article with sidebars, which can be a chart, a graph, or a bullet-list of your major points. If you can think of anything that might fit into a sidebar format, be sure to tell the editor.

2.1.b What should your submission look like?

Unless you have received instructions otherwise, most editors want to receive typewritten, double-spaced copy. They may even specify the font (Times New Union seems quite popular). You should number each page, either with your pagination program or by typing the number or, if necessary, by neatly handprinting the number at the bottom of each page. Allow margins that are wide enough so that a person could write comments down the side of a page.

Enclose a cover letter with your manuscript, addressed to the individual who hired you. It need not be lengthy and can be along the lines of "I have completed the article that you requested on exercise for dogs [or whatever the topic] and it is enclosed for your review." The next paragraph can be a simple "Thank you," followed by your name. Use letterhead (discussed in chapter 13). This will help the editor remember who you are, how your name is spelled, and, very importantly, where to send the money.

Writer's guidelines

Most magazines have writer's guidelines that are available for the asking. If you are interested in writing for a particular publication, call and ask for a copy of its writer's guidelines. With these in hand, you have another tool to better tailor your query to their needs.

Also ask if you can receive their editorial schedule for any special topics they have planned for future issues.

freelance facts

2.1.c Kill fees

Once in a while an editor may hire you to write an article and then decide that the article doesn't work. The editor may acknowledge that you did a good job, but for some reason he or she cannot use the piece. Perhaps the focus of the magazine has changed and your article is no longer suitable.

In situations like this, "kill fees" are paid. A kill fee is a percentage of the agreed-upon amount for an accepted article. If the kill fee is 20% and you were supposed to receive $300 for the article, then you will receive a $60 kill fee if the editor chooses not to publish it.

You may well be able to sell the article intact to another editor and thus be ahead by $60, but it's important to review any contract between you and the original publication before you assume that it's okay to do so. There may be a clause saying that you can't resell the piece, even if it's not published.

Sometimes editors include specific provisions for kill fees in contracts and sometimes they do not. Even if your agreement had no mention of a kill fee, it doesn't hurt to ask for one should the editor decide against publication and you acted in good faith and, as far as you can determine, fulfilled your agreement. The editor may say no. Then again, he or she may say yes.

---

freelance facts

Payment on acceptance vs. payment on publication

Payment on acceptance means that the editor will pay you once he or she decides the article will be published. This is usually (but not always) before publication.

Payment on publication means that you will be paid after the article is published, which may mean 30 days afterward or later.

Most writers prefer payment on acceptance because they get their money faster. But some magazines refuse to pay on acceptance, so you may need to accept payment on publication if you want to write for them.

2.2 Writing for newspapers

Newspapers already have reporters on staff to cover the major stories in the area. A freelancer may be able to break into freelance writing in the "lifestyle" part of the newspaper, where many different topics are covered. Stories in this section need not be as timely as news stories. This means the editor can use your article next week or next month.

2.2.a How do you break into newspaper writing?

As with magazine writing, the way to break into newspaper writing is to write a query to the editor of the section of the newspaper that interests you, describing your idea and why you are the right person to write the piece. If you think the idea is really hot, you can call the editor; however, be prepared to be put off if the editor is "on deadline" or under pressure for some other reason.

Also, as with magazine writing, if the editor wants to hire you, he or she will tell you how much to write, when it's due, and how much the newspaper will pay. Actually, the editor may "forget" the how-much-to-pay part. If that happens, you will need to ask about payment.

Newspaper people generally think in "column inches," so when the editor tells you the length of article to write, he or she will tell you to write X column inches. If you ask how many words that is, you will usually get a baffled response. It's not hard to figure out for yourself. Go look at the newspaper you want to write for and measure off a square inch. Then count how many words are in that square inch. If it's 100 words per square inch and the editor wants ten column inches, your article should be about 1,000 words. If you continue to write for newspapers, after awhile you will start thinking in column inches.

Newspaper editors may want you to e-mail them your copy. Several years ago, when I wrote articles for my local paper, I e-mailed them directly to the editor's computer, where she edited my work on her computer and then submitted it as copy for the paper.

Don't expect newspapers to show you the edited version of your work. Often it doesn't occur to them to do so, and other times they are on a tight deadline and don't have time to run it by you.

If it's a slow news day or your piece is extremely compelling, the editor can choose to publish it right away.

Newspapers usually don't pay very well, so you could receive less than $100, depending on the newspaper or the story itself.

2.2.b Newspaper syndicates

It's a very tight market, but you may also be able to sell your ideas to a newspaper syndicate. *Writer's Market* lists a variety of possibilities.

A newspaper syndicate is an organization that creates features of varying lengths, which are then sold to many different newspapers (and sometimes magazines) nationwide. Much of the material you read in large newspapers comes from syndicates such as the Associated Press or the Creator's Syndicate. Syndicates also sell regular columns, such as "Dear Abby," the cartoon "For Better or For Worse," and so forth.

Sometimes syndicates are interested in fresh and timely pieces and may be willing to try you out — usually they will ask you to work "on spec" until they get to know you. That means they will ask you to write a piece, but will not commit to publishing it (or paying you for it) until they read it.

In addition, sometimes you can resell a magazine feature to a newspaper syndicate. I resold my magazine feature on single parents in the military to a newspaper syndicate. The editor knew it had already been published because I sent him a photocopy of the article when I asked if he was interested. But it was too long. The editor asked if I could cut it down to 30% of its original size? I could and did.

2.3 Does writing for magazines and newspapers mean you have to write for nickels and dimes?

One myth about writing is that you always have to start at the bottom of the pay scale. In fact, many writers have recommended that new writers should start with the lowest-paying markets and slowly work their way up.

My question is: why? I don't understand this advice at all. Instead, I recommend starting with the highest paying market and working your way down. Just because you're new doesn't mean major publishers will automatically reject your ideas. What matters to them is the idea first and your credibility second. If you are a newbie with a fantastic idea and you can convince an editor you can carry the idea off, you do have a chance. Years ago I wrote an article on children's computer software for *McCall's* magazine. I got the contract because the editors knew very little about the subject but perceived it was "hot," and they knew I had written many reviews of educational programs for computer magazines.

New writers may be inexperienced, but they may also be good writers with great ideas. Why deprive the better-paying markets of the chance to publish your work? If they pass up the opportunity, then you can work your way downward to the lower-paying markets.

Writing for magazines can be a lucrative and glamorous way to make a living as a freelancer, but many writers think writing and publishing books is the height of glamor. I will cover the book market in the next chapter. Be sure to read it if you have ever had any interest in writing a book for publication.

A small newspaper is not going to pay major league dollars, and a high-circulation magazine is likely to pay well — but there are many other factors to consider. For example, if you can churn out copy at a rapid rate, you may make as much from lower paying markets as a writer who sells one piece to a high-paying publication.

CHAPTER 5

Writing Books

Writing books — how glamorous, how exciting! And it *is* very exciting when your book is printed and you are holding it in your hands, marveling that all your work has been encapsulated into this one solid object that you hope many people will wish to also hold and read.

However, arriving at that point requires a lot of work. Authoring books is different in many ways from writing magazine articles, press releases, or any other form of writing. This chapter covers the basics on writing books, such as how to write a book proposal, what to do if you get an offer, and what you need to know about literary agents. But first, I'd like to start by clearing up some misconceptions about writing books.

1. Myths and realities of writing books

There are many misconceptions about what it's like to write a book. The four most common myths about writing books are listed below:

- Writing a book is a good way to get rich fast.

- It takes years (or at least one year) to write a book.

The entire book should be written before it's submitted to anyone.

Fame is inevitable and people will really appreciate your work.

As the author of 15 books myself, and as a person with many friends who are authors, I can (and will) tell you about the way it usually is.

1.1 Get rich quick by writing books?

You don't have to starve to death if you concentrate on writing books. But don't think that writing books will provide you with an opulent lifestyle and transform your normal-looking surroundings into a palatial estate. That almost never happens. In order to make money writing books, you have to keep your expenses down, obtain as much of an advance as you can, and write at least two and preferably more books per year — unless your advance for one book was very generous. (I'll talk more about advances later in this chapter.)

1.2 Spend years on books?

Ann Douglas, a Canadian author of ten books including *The Unofficial Guide to Having a Baby* (Macmillan, 1999), says it takes her two to three months to write a book and four months to write a long book. Ann is a little faster than I am — I need about three to four months to research and write a self-help book. Both of us work full time, which sometimes means nights, weekends, and holidays. But spend a whole year on one book? I shudder at the thought.

1.3 Don't write the entire manuscript before submission

A major mistake of the novice author is writing the whole book before showing it to anyone. Instead, you should write a book proposal — which I'll discuss later in this chapter — and one or two chapters. That's it! If you write more, you are wasting your time. What if no one wants the book and you spent all that time writing it? Time is money!

Another reason you should write only part of the book is that if an editor is interested, he or she may want it written with a particular slant that hasn't occurred to you or may point out the need for chapters that

> Most publishers will not wait an entire year for a manuscript. The average amount of time an author has to deliver an average-sized book is six months. And he or she is usually working on another book within that timeframe.

you haven't written. You might have to dump large portions of your already-written manuscript, and think how painful that would be!

> Author Ann Douglas says she doesn't write more than a few chapters until she has an advance check in her hand. Not just a contract — an actual check. I agree completely. In fact, even after I sign a contract, I don't believe the book is "real" until I can see the check for myself. Then I know it's time to start seriously working on the book.

1.4 Fame is not inevitable for authors

I don't want to discourage you by telling you that you'll do all this work to write a book that nobody will read. Au contraire! Many people are likely to read your book, especially if you perform some basic book promotions, such as telling everyone you know about your book, offering yourself as an interviewee to local newspapers and television stations, and getting your name out there in front of the public.

But do discard the "better mousetrap" idea. This is the (wrong) idea that if you do a really great job (or invent a better mousetrap), everyone will know about it. With the many events swirling around in today's society, people who may be interested in your book may never hear about it unless it is brought to their attention.

This is not a book about book promotion, so I don't have the space to go on at length on this topic; however, I can tell you that your publisher may have some good ideas about promotion. You may have some ideas yourself. If you come up with an idea your publisher hasn't thought of, that doesn't mean it is a bad idea. It merely means that the publisher hasn't thought of it — so suggest it.

> I have promoted my books by doing author interviews on Amazon.com, appearing on television and radio shows, writing letters to the editor that mention my book, and using many other tactics. In a few cases, I have even arranged with the publisher to sell my book myself to specialized audiences.

2. Literary agents: The 15% solution

A literary agent is a person who works for an agency (it can be a one-person agency) and who represents authors to publishers. Many publishers refuse to look at unsolicited queries or proposals, so getting a contract with a major publisher on your own is unlikely. Success is certainly not guaranteed with an agent, but the odds are much improved.

For his or her efforts, the agent receives a percentage of what the author is paid. That may be 10%, but is more likely to be 15%.

There are good, mediocre, and bad literary agents. It is unwise to sign up with an agent just because he or she is willing to take you on. It's better to ask for the agent's client list and to call some of the writers on this list. Ask them about how well they have done since they signed on with the agent you are considering.

I have had three agents. The first was a very competent woman who negotiated an excellent contract for a nonfiction book for me. So why wasn't she a keeper? Because I subsequently learned that her true interest was fiction and, in particular, selling romance novels. Not my interest at all. She and I parted amicably and still communicate.

The second agent experience wasn't so happy, what with lost proposals I submitted (repeatedly!) and other problems.

My current agent is the best fit for me because he agents mostly nonfiction and is aggressive without being too pushy. He is also knowledgeable and intuitive about many facets of publishing.

In some cases in the past, and also in cases when I work on ghost-writing projects, I negotiate my own contracts. If a contract is very complex (or if I am being hired by an attorney), then I also consult an attorney who is familiar with book publishing.

When dealing with major publishers, I like the middleman aspect that an agent brings. If a publisher starts to pressure you to take a lower price or meet an unrealistic deadline, you can tell him or her to talk to your agent.

2.1 Finding an agent

How can you find a literary agent who is right for you? I think the best reference guide for someone seeking a literary agent is the *Writer's Guide*

> It can be very comforting to hide behind your agent and let him or her be the "bad guy." A good agent doesn't mind playing this role and may in fact relish it.

to Book Editors, Publishers, and Literary Agents by Jeff Herman. Prima Publishing puts out a new edition every year. (See the Appendix for further information.) This book lists agencies and addresses and provides the names and interests of particular agents, with information on books they have sold in the past. This may allow you to match your interests with prospects in this book.

2.2 What should you ask a prospective agent?

The first question you should ask an agent is if he or she is accepting new clients who are outstanding writers. (Meaning you, of course.) If the answer is "yes" or "maybe," then continue with more questions.

Here are some questions that can help you narrow down the list of possible agents. Be sure to add your own questions to this list and delete any that don't work for you.

- Will you represent first-time authors with good book proposals? Remember, agents want book proposals, as do book editors.

- What percentage of your book contracts are nonfiction? Fiction?

- What kind of help do you provide to your authors? Some may read proposals for free and offer suggestions. A few agents charge a "reading fee." In general, it is best to avoid those who charge reading fees.

- What major publishers have you obtained contracts with over the past year? Ask for the past year because over the course of five or ten years, nearly anyone could place at least a few books with major publishers. You're interested in now.

- About how long does your average client stay with you? The agent may not know the exact answer, but he or she should be able to give you a rough estimate. If the average client stays for years, that's good.

- Do you have a Web site? A Web site may provide you with valuable information, such as a list of the writers this agent represents (they should be current clients; if it's not clear, ask the agent), and publishers the agent has worked with recently.

2.3 What should you ask an agent's clients?

If the agent sounds promising, contact at least two or three of his or her current clients.

The following is a list of questions you might consider asking writer clients of an agent:

- 📖 How long have you been working with this agent?

- 📖 Did you have any other agents before? (If not, the writer has no basis for comparison, and that should be factored into your evaluation.)

- 📖 Has your agent been able to obtain contracts with any major publishers for you?

- 📖 Do you feel comfortable with him/her?

2.4 Think about who is paying the bills

It is important to keep in mind that even though the agent is *your* agent, most are really concerned with pleasing the publishers — especially the publishers with the money. The agent wants to have a continuing and happy relationship with major publishers. So don't presume that an agent is concerned with your interests solely. That would be naive.

This does not mean you should not work with a literary agent, any more than it means you should never engage the services of a realtor. Agents can open important doors for you. Contracts with agents vary greatly. If possible, you should try to get a per-book contract. If you sign a time-limited contract, try to limit the time period to no more than one year.

2.5 What does your agent do when you receive an offer?

When you are offered a contract by a publisher, your agent reviews it, makes a recommendation to you, and then lets you decide whether to accept or reject the offer. He or she will usually tell you what the basic terms are, including the amount of the advance, the royalty percentage, and the due date. (Your agent should provide you with more information than that, but those are the three items that I want to know before I decide to accept an offer.)

Often the agent will negotiate changes in the contract to make it more favorable to you. Once the publisher, the agent, and you are in agreement on basic terms and conditions, the contract is drawn up. The agent receives it and checks it to make sure it's okay, then forwards the contract to you for signing.

Be sure to read your contract! Even though it is probably okay, you should not sign any contract, ever, without first reading it.

2.6 Selling a book yourself (without an agent)

If you don't have an agent and don't want to (or can't) get one, you may wish to sell your book on your own. You will still need a book proposal, however, so be sure to read the section that follows this one very carefully.

How do you sell a book on your own? You write a query letter (see chapter 7). Send this letter to the editor at the publishing house you have decided is right for your book.

I recommend you buy a copy of the most recent edition of the *Writer's Guide to Book Editors, Publishers, and Literary Agents*, by Jeff Herman. This book provides publishers in the United States and Canada and includes the names of editors and their addresses. Even better, many editors provide comments describing the topics that particularly interest them, so you can target your query to a specific editor. Just page through and look at the various listings, highlighting or underlining names of editors who might be interested in your book. (It is okay to mark up a book that belongs to you, though it may seem sacrilegious the first time that you do it!)

Should you send out only one letter? You can, but that could drag things out for months. Do what literary agents do: they send the letter out to ten or more publishers simultaneously to solicit interest in your book.

If and when an editor at a publishing house wants to see your proposal, send it right out. Do not expect an offer within a week or two. The person may not even read the proposal in that timeframe. It can take months before you hear anything.

Before sending a query letter, call the publisher to make sure the editor is still with the firm. If so, then proceed!

Should you hire an agent? This is a question too individual and too difficult to explore in this book. Many people are very successful without agents while others swear they would be nowhere had it not been for the valuable assistance of their agent.

3. The advance

If you are working with a literary agent, you can assume you will receive an advance because agents won't work for free. An advance is an advance against royalties — whatever money you receive will be deducted from income you earn from sales of your book.

The check for the advance is sent to your agent and, in fact, is written to him or her. Your agent cashes the check, keeping his or her agreed-upon percentage, and then remits a check for the balance to you. The agent should send your money to you within a week or two after he or she receives the check.

After the book is published, you will start receiving royalty statements every six months. These show how your book is selling. They will also show how much of your advance you have earned back and how much (if anything) the publisher owes you.

Publishers often pay half the advance upon signing and the other half when the job is done, but other arrangements may be made.

Let's take a simple case as an example. Say you received a $5,000 advance and are paid a royalty of 10% of the list price of a book. If the book is sold for $10, you will receive a royalty of $1 per book. This means that the publisher needs to sell 5,000 books before it owes you any money — before you earn out your advance payment.

If the publisher sells 10,000 books, it will owe you $5,000 because you already received $5,000 in the advance. Of that $5,000, your agent will receive at least 10%, or $500. This means your agent owes you $4,500.

Book advances generally do not include expenses. They are flat fees, and the writer who takes on a book project should consider any anticipated expenses before signing a contract.

This is a very simple example, and there are all sorts of complicated formulas that publishers may use to calculate royalties. They may base the royalties on "net sales" instead of the list price of the book. They may hold back a "reserve for returns," which is a percentage of net sales or some other number.

If you decide to end your relationship with your agent, he or she will still receive royalty checks for the books that you worked on together and will continue to forward the money, less his or her percentage, to you.

As you can see, your agent must be a person you can trust and have a good working relationship with. He or she need not be your best friend, but there should be a certain camaraderie.

4. The book proposal

A book proposal is a written description of the topic that you want to write about. It includes specific elements, such as information about you, the prospective author, and an analysis of the competition.

4.1 Why write a book proposal?

Book proposals are important tools to sell your book for a variety of reasons:

- The majority of editors and agents won't look at your book without a proposal.

- Writing a book proposal forces you to focus on your future readers.

- The book proposal enables you to get a feel for whether this project is doable and whether you really want to go forward with it.

4.1.a Editors and agents want proposals, not books

Editors and also agents want manuscripts that will sell. Your finished book alone cannot tell them what they need to know about who will read your book and why, and what books are competition to your book. A book proposal can.

Another reason editors and agents want proposals is that usually one person alone cannot make the decision to buy, particularly at a medium-sized or major publisher. Instead, many companies hold editorial meetings at which an advocate for your book will present the case

Your book proposal should do everything possible to present a convincing case that your book is highly saleable.

that it should be purchased. The proposal will serve two purposes for the editor who loves your book idea:

(a) The editor can draw information from it to present a strong case.

(b) The editor can pass out copies of the proposal itself.

4.1.b Writing a proposal helps you define readers

When you write a book without first preparing a proposal, you usually ignore some important data that would help you write a better book.

For example, an integral part of a book proposal is an analysis of the market, including the demographics of who is most likely to buy your book. A classic error is to say that everyone over the age of 18 will love your book. That is almost never true — few books appeal to a general audience of all adults of all ages and backgrounds.

Instead, you must determine who your target markets are and explain why they are your targets. For example, when I prepared the proposal for my book *The Unofficial Guide to Eldercare*, I knew the target market was women in their forties and fifties because it is they who are the primary caregivers to older people. Sure, some men take care of their elderly parents, but they don't predominate. (I'll talk more about this aspect when I discuss the elements of the book proposal.)

The proposal also forces you to take a look at your competition because you must write about how your book will be different and better than the other books that currently exist. Identifying and analyzing these books will improve your feel for the market as well.

4.1.c Writing a proposal helps you decide whether to go ahead with a book

I have written a few proposals and decided not to write the book. Why? Because the subject would have required much more research than I felt I had time for or because I didn't think I'd receive enough advance money to cover the research time.

Before writing the proposal and doing the research, the book idea seemed ingenious and wonderful. Then I checked out the subject in more depth, looked at the competition, and decided..."Forget it! This topic is not worth it." I invested a few weeks researching and writing the proposal. But if I had gone ahead with the project without writing the proposal, I would have spent six months or more on a book that would have made me miserable. Writing the proposal sounds like a good investment to me.

On other occasions, the research and writing of a proposal have made it clear that there is a strong market for a book and that I can do the topic within a reasonable time.

> Each person must decide for himself or herself whether a particular book project is worth proceeding on. And the book proposal can help you focus on making the right decision for yourself.

4.2 The elements of a proposal

Following are the basic elements of a book proposal that you should be sure to include:

(a) An overview of the project

(b) A description of prospective readers (the "market")

(c) Information on competing books

(d) An author biography

(e) Specifications

(f) An outline

(g) Sample chapter(s)

> Do not assume that your editor, let's call him "Mr. Ed," understands anything whatsoever about your topic. He's probably a smart guy and a college graduate, but he may never have heard of your subject. Be sure to explain details that may be unknown to him and define any terminology that could be considered insider jargon. Mr. Ed may turn out to be an "insider" himself and to be fascinated by your topic, but assume that he is totally ignorant. Of course, you will not talk down to him. He's not stupid.

4.2.a The overview

The overview should be an attention-grabber that shows your reader (an editor) why your idea is a good one. You can start with an anecdote, a quotation, or an intriguing fact and build from there. Don't rely on *telling* the reader this book is needed: show why it's necessary.

Sample 1 shows a portion of the opening of a proposal I wrote and subsequently sold.

4.2.b The market

The market refers to the people who will read this book, including primary and secondary markets. Here is where you need to put yourself in the shoes of other people, your future readers.

Most authors think their books are needed and deal with very exciting topics, otherwise why would they want to write them? But your challenge is to convince an editor who is neutral about the topic. *Prove* to Ms. Anthrope (the editor) as effectively as you can that those readers are out there and they will need and want your book.

The primary market is of course the people you believe will be your main readers, the ones you are aiming your book at. Be as specific as you possibly can by asking yourself the following questions:

> Use statistics, anecdotes, logical deductions, or whatever else it takes to create a compelling argument that there are groups of people who will need and want your book.

- Are your readers male, female, or both? If both, what is the mix? 60/40, favoring males, or the other way around? Why?

- How old are the readers? Give a range of no more than 10 years whenever possible. No one expects you to say your target reader is a 46-year-old woman (although I was able to say that once, based on a study I cited). This information is important because the 25-year-old man or woman is different from the 45-year-old in many ways, just as the 25-year-old man is different in many ways from the 25-year-old woman.

- What is the socioeconomic status of your readers? Are they wealthy or are they middle class? They better not be poor. Poor people do not buy books in bookstores. They may read them in the library, but they can't afford to buy a lot of books. An editor told me once that she received a great proposal on helpful hints for homeless people. But homeless people don't buy books. So she turned it down.

Overview From a Book Proposal

Target market was Americans but I have since written about adoption for Canadians. Note: Whenever you can use a number that sounds impressive, do so.

About 110,000 children are adopted each year by Americans, and in the overwhelming majority of cases, the children are adopted by a married couple. This means that nearly a quarter of a million adults are directly affected by adoption annually as they become adoptive parents.

It's also true that there are many more people who consider adoption each year, and some experts estimate that at least two or three million people each year are seriously weighing whether they should adopt a child. They haven't applied to an adoption agency or sought out the services of an adoption attorney, and they haven't joined an adoptive parent group. They really haven't done anything at all — except to consider the possibility of what it would be like to adopt a child and if adoption would be the right choice for their family.

Note: Who are these people? What is their problem? Those are the issues mentioned above.

The problem is, they really don't know how to look at themselves and their own lives to evaluate whether adoption might be right for them. Nor do they know how or where to seek out formal and informal information on adoption — information that could help them decide whether or not they should take that first step leading toward adopting a child. And this is because there is no guide for people who are unsure about whether or not adoption would work for them.

The few books on adoption that are published by major publishers concentrate on the how-to of actually adopting an infant or older child, but all of them include the underlying assumption that the reader already knows that he or she is ready to adopt now. I think this is a backward way to deal with such a very difficult decision as to whether a person should adopt a child or not. If you are uncertain yet interested in adoption, you don't need to know how to find an agency

Note: The above includes a general comment on competition and why this book is needed.

or what a home study investigation is like because you have not yet reached that point where you would become actively involved in the adoption process.

Compare adoption to another key institution in our society: marriage. If you are unsure of marriage but are trying to seriously consider whether it's right for you, a book on how to plan your wedding would be very inappropriate and unhelpful, because the wedding book author assumes you already know you want to get married. In the same way, how-to books on adoption make the same assumption – that the readers already know that they want to adopt.

End of my hard sell. From there I moved on to issues and questions that needed to be answered.

Yet this is not true for many people, who are unsure about whether or not they should adopt a child – just as many people aren't clear on whether marriage is a good choice for them at a given time in their lives. As a result, what is really needed is a kind of "prequel" to the existing how-to adoption books, and *Before You Adopt* will fill this important role.

- Once you've stated what you believe is the socioeconomic status of your primary readers, explain why you think this. How do you know?

- How many people are there in the market you're describing? No one expects you to say there are 2,374,888 readers who need and will want this book. But give some sort of range whenever possible. If the book is aimed at a certain kind of hobbyist, you might be able to get an estimate of the number of hobbyists of this kind from a national organization. If you do get such a number, be sure to include it! "The National Association of Jumping Beans in Chicago, Illinois, says that over 3 million people collect jumping beans..."

- Everyone in the group you've defined won't buy your book, so give a realistic estimate of purchasers — say, 1% to 5% of the total number or whatever seems right to you — and cite that number. For example, "If just 1% of the National Association of Jumping

Beans members bought my thrilling new book about beans in the new millennium, that would mean 30,000 readers!"

Fatal mistake: Do not state that everyone, everywhere will love your book. This is the mark of the rank amateur and it makes editors crazy. It would be great if your book turned out to be a bestseller. But you can't assume that bestselling status is a "given" in your proposal. Editors need to provide evidence there are at least 5,000 to 10,000 buyers, including all markets, to justify publishing a book. You must present that hard evidence in your proposal.

You should also include descriptive information about your target readers. Are they military veterans? Are they collectors?

Information on gender, age, and socioeconomic status; the approximate number of readers; and unique traits of your target readers are all elements that should be in the market section of your proposal. You can add other data that you think is important, but don't leave any of these out. If you're not sure about some aspect of your market, make an educated guess that you can back up with a logical argument.

Your secondary markets are important too. Who are they — social workers? Libraries? Physicians? And why do you think these groups would be interested? A few paragraphs on the secondary markets and why they would want your book will suffice. Editors love the idea of making quantity sales to more than one group.

Libraries are an especially good market to include as a secondary, and most editors know this. Decide whether your book would appeal more to public libraries, public school libraries, college libraries, or some other kind of library and explain why.

4.2.c The competition

The competition section of your proposal needs to be very strong. No matter how wonderful your idea is, the editor won't buy your book if he or she thinks there are other books out there that are just as good. You must convince the editor, in your discussion of the competition, that your book will be different and better. Just saying it will be unique is not enough. You must *show* how it will be different.

First you must find out who *are* your competitors. There are several ways to discover which books are most closely competitive to the book you are proposing.

(a) *The bookstore.* Most authors love visiting bookstores. I do! The first thing you do, of course, is to make sure they have any of your existing books in stock. If they do, you're happy, although not completely happy unless the front cover is showing (if it's not showing, rearrange the shelves so it is). If they're not there, you assume that they've sold all the copies and ask a clerk to make sure more are on order.

Next on your agenda is to visit the section of the bookstore where your new book would appear. There you pull out the already published books that you will compete against and take a look at them. See who published them and what the cover looks like, and skim the contents. If you think the book represents serious competition, you may decide to buy it to analyze it further.

Bookstores are a good place to look for competing books, but they don't stock every book that might compete with yours, and they might have sold out of a book that could be competitive. Do not assume, when you enter the bookstore, that their stock is all there is. It isn't.

(b) *The library.* You might also decide to visit your local library. Libraries are a wealth of information and you really should befriend your reference librarian. Most reference librarians are curious and helpful people and they like the idea of helping an author.

Check the books in your library that might compete with your future book. The good news is you won't have to buy them. The bad news is that they may have a very limited selection and little or nothing on your topic.

(c) *Books in Print.* While you're at the library, check *Books in Print.* That's a hefty set of reference books that is usually behind or somewhere near the reference librarian's desk. The volumes list — what else? — books that are in print. There's a subject volume and several others. Haul those books over to a table and find your subject. Make notes listing the titles that may be your book's competitors. Take into consideration the date published. If the book was published in 1970, few publishers would consider it competition for a new book. My personal cutoff is about seven or eight years earlier.

The disadvantage of using *Books in Print* is that you have to go to the library, write things down, and then figure out how to get the books. I rarely use this strategy anymore, but I think everyone should try it at least once.

(d) *The Internet.* My personal favorite place to search is Amazon.com on the Internet (www.amazon.com/exec/obidos/ats-query-page). You can search by subject or author, and this amazing database does appear to list every book in print. When I am considering a topic, I search by subject and then look at all the titles that have popped up in my search. Each book has its own page, which includes important data such as price, publisher, and date published. Many book pages include descriptions of the book. I usually print out pages of books that I think could be competitors.

The disadvantage of Amazon.com is that when you do your search, you may find that there are a hundred or more titles on your subject and you could easily become discouraged. However, as you wade through the list you may find that many of the books were written ten or more years ago and were published by No-Name Publishers or Tiny Press. Major publishers would not consider them to be competitors. Take the time to do a thorough check.

Price is also a consideration when checking out competitors. One editor pointed out several books she thought could be competition for my manuscript. I easily demolished her fears by using Amazon.com — for example, one of the books was not only old, but the price was $87.50. The editor and I both knew my proposed book would price out at $25.00, tops.

(e) *People in the field.* Another good tactic to find books that might compete with yours is to ask people in the field what books they would recommend on this topic. They may turn out to be obscure books or out of print but they may also be serious competitors.

Try to find at least four or five books that could be considered competition to your book. If you can't find that many, you are either not looking hard enough or there are very few people who are interested in this topic.

It need not be an exact competitor but at least should be in the ballpark. For example, if you want to write about Greek statues and can find only one or two books on this topic (I'm sure you could find more — this is just an example), then look at the broader topic of Greek art or Greek culture. Try to stay as close to your topic as you can.

Once you've narrowed down your selection, you will need to read the books yourself, whether you borrow them from a library or a friend or buy them. You cannot critique a book unless you read it. I often like to buy the books I plan to critique because then I can mark them up with underlinings and bend over pages that I want to return to. If you can't buy the book or don't want to, you may decide to photocopy those pages that will help you write your competition section.

Read the books with the eyes and mindset of the prospective reader. Ask yourself the following questions as you read:

- Does the language seem appropriate for the audience? If the author seems to be targeting high school graduates, is he or she using words that would require readers to have a dictionary by their side? Or is the author writing too simplistically, even patronizingly? Readers don't like to be talked down to. In my proposals, I have cited long and boring passages as examples of why a competing book is not a concern, at the same time, assuring the editor I would not talk down to my readers.

- Does the author deliver what was promised in the title and in the introduction? Or does he or she veer off into the stratosphere, talking about irrelevant boring details. I criticized one book with a lengthy passage on 17th-century medical practices. A few details would have been relevant, but not pages and pages, especially since that author shortchanged readers who desperately needed information about the topic of medical practices today.

- Alternatively, does the author skim the surface of the topic and leave you feeling as if you didn't learn much?

- Check the index. (If there isn't one, this lack may be a point to criticize.) Did the author cover topics that you think are important? If so, read those entries. They may be adequate and may not. If not, that's a point to criticize. If the author didn't cover them at all, that's also worth criticizing.

- Look at the price of the book. Even if it's a wonderful book, will many people buy it at its price? Remember the book that could potentially have competed with mine, which was no longer competitive when the editor heard its high price.

- Is the author an expert on the subject or does he or she have a coauthor or someone who writes a foreword who is an expert? Find out.

- Who published this book? If the publisher was John Wiley & Sons, they are major contenders in the publishing world. If it was published by Mary Ellen Press (a name I made up), it is not a major contender. You still should mention the "Mary Ellen" book in your competition writeup, but the nobody publisher is a plus for you.

- What about the length of book? Is it too short? Too long?

Once you've done the research on your competition, you're ready to start writing. What information should you include? Be sure that you provide the exact name of each title, the author or authors' names, the publisher, and the year of publication. This is essential information. Write no more than three quarters of a double-spaced page on each book. Sometimes a paragraph will suffice, but not if the book is a major contender.

Start with the most serious competitor first and describe the book. You need not be venomous, although I have hovered on that line myself. State what the author attempted to do and how he or she performed the task.

Should you abandon all hope if several major publishers have relatively recent books on your topic? No. Review those books and decide how yours would be different and better. Be as specific as possible.

Never praise a book that represents competition to your book. If another book is so great, why does the world need yours? At most, you can say that a competing book does an adequate job of (whatever it does an adequate job of), but that it is lacking in the area of (whatever it is lacking in) and your book will remedy that omission by providing readers with this important information that was missing in the other book.

When you really get into the spirit of this, it becomes easy to see major flaws in other books. Let's face it, any book can be criticized. Some of them, however, cry out to be denounced. I found some sexist remarks in one book that a competitor wrote, and you can be sure that I brought that to the attention of a feminist editor.

Explain how your book will be different and better but keep the information on your book to a minimum — a sentence or two per each competitive book.

The following are some common mistakes writers make when they write about the competition for their proposed book:

(a) *Not finding books by major publishers.* Editors *will* check, and if they find you haven't done your homework, that will turn them off.

(b) *Being too nice to the competition.* Again, do *not* praise other people's books! You don't have to be nasty. But you shouldn't be too nice. I read a proposal written by a doctor who rhapsodized on and on about someone else's book. I asked the doctor what we needed his book for if this other one was so great, and he began telling me about the problem areas and the missing points in the other man's book. I stopped him and said, "Okay, don't tell me anymore. Put that information in your proposal."

(c) *Overdoing it.* A few times I have seen proposals in which the competition is denounced too stridently. The book may be flawed, but we really should not launch the author off on a one-way trip into space because of his or her miserable and failed attempts with this book. Even if you think so, don't say it.

(d) *Relying on jargon.* The editor may be an expert on Pre-Columbian artifacts, but probably he or she is not. This is why you should use everyday language. Explain any terms that you really need to use and that someone might not be familiar with.

Does this sound like hard work? It is, but once you get into the spirit of the project and learn what your competitors have done, you can begin to see more clearly how you can create a book that fulfills the needs of readers. And you can begin to shape that book in your mind.

You may find that what you thought would be your primary thrust has been thoroughly covered by Author X. But what he or she doesn't cover, and is really important, is _____. You see how your book will need to emphasize that topic.

As you critique your competitors, your own book becomes more alive and real to you. It is quite an exciting process!

A book proposal is a sales vehicle. Does Coke tell the world that Pepsi is pretty good? I don't think so!

Read your section on competition aloud, either to yourself or to someone else. When you read something aloud, flaws become more readily apparent. You may hear them yourself or the person you are reading to may get a very puzzled look on his or her face. Make necessary changes to your proposal.

4.2.d About the author

This section is where many people fall flat on their face — even more often than they err on the too-kind side in the "Competition" section. Can you guess what error most authors make here? If you guessed that authors are too *unkind* to themselves and too modest, then you win the prize!

Most of us believe modesty is a positive trait, that we should be virtuous and good and not brag about our achievements too much because it's not seemly or polite. Throw those thoughts out the window when it comes to the "About the Author" section of your proposal.

Tell yourself that you are the only person who can write this book. If necessary, make this your mantra and repeat it mentally and out loud: "I am the only person who can write the true story of whatever."

Other people might be able to write books on your topic, but not in the specific way you will, and not with your plan and your knowledge and abilities. You are The One.

As the old song says, "You have to accentuate the positive, eliminate the negative, and don't mess with Mr. In-Between." The primary purpose of the author section is to sell yourself to the editor. This takes some thought.

First, think about your past achievements, whether or not they have anything to do with the book you want to write, and list them. (It might help to review your resume and see what you've listed there.)

What kind of achievements? There's enormous variability here. If you are a college graduate, that alone is an achievement. If you are an editor or writer now, or if you have ever done anything in the writing profession, including copy editing (some people might not think that counts, but I'd count it if I'd ever done it), then write that down. (If you are not a college graduate or have never had anything published, you *will not* say that in your "About the Author" section.)

How specific you should be about previous writing credits depends on their applicability to the book. For example, if you wrote an article once about how to plan a block party, and your book will be on the war in Bosnia, you probably won't mention your earlier subject. You'll just say that you've written articles in the past. Close enough.

Have you ever received an award? Many people have attained some accolades but have forgotten about them or thought they were unimportant. No previous award is too insignificant to consider. You may decide not to include it. But at least consider it. For example, I always mention that I received an Air Force Commendation Medal when I was in the military. I don't say what it was for because nobody cares. It just *sounds* good to have gotten one.

I am not attempting to transform you into some kind of egomaniac. But in the author section you will provide every conceivable reason why it's you who must write this book. If there are any possible negative areas, you should either ignore them or turn them into strengths. For example, let's say you are living in another country. An editor might worry about your researching capability. So you explain how, in your unique position in Wherever, you not only have easy access to data on the Internet, but you also travel to the United States twice a year, or you explain how you are in close contact with the United States because...and give the reasons. If you can't think of any negative aspects that are relevant, then don't worry about it.

> When my 19-year-old son asked me what to say in a job interview if a potential employer asked him what his weak points were, I told him to transform weak points into strengths. For example, let's say you are detail oriented and rather obsessive-compulsive. I would present these traits by saying that I become so immersed in a job that I sometimes don't notice that it's lunchtime or 5:00 p.m. because I want to do a really good job and get it done on time. Think about how you might use this approach.

Try to create tie-ins between yourself and the topic. If you can, allude to any relevant facts that you can link to your topic, no matter how tenuous the link. For example, if you want to write a travelogue about Japan and the only link you can think of is that you have been to Japan several times, put that in! Many people have never been to Japan, and you have a first-person perspective. It's not necessary to mention that you were there a decade ago unless an editor specifically asks when you were there.

Let's say you wrack your brains and can think of *no* possible tie-in between the topic and you. Then you could say that you are fascinated by this topic — which, presumably, you are — and want to mobilize your enthusiasm, knowledge, and background to create a very good book. Actually, I'd say that anyway, even if I have many different ways to link myself to the topic. Enthusiasm is a much under-rated virtue. If combined with the virtue of Persistence, the two together move mountains.

Can't dump the shy you? Don't despair if you're still having trouble writing about You the Wonderful. This problem occurs frequently. Here is my solution — and it sounds totally off the wall, but it does work for many people. Pretend that you are writing about a person who is just like you and is someone you like. This person clearly deserves the best possible writeup. So look at yourself as if you are an admiring third party. It works! I find I'm able to write about my best achievements and successes with no further difficulty. You may even want to try this if you don't think you have a modesty problem. The results may surprise you. (It also works well for writing resumes.)

What about other credentials?

(a) Do describe your academic background if you are a college graduate. All you need to say is that you received a B.A. in Animal Husbandry from the University of New Hampshire in 19xx. If you have any graduate degrees, Ph.D.s, or M.D.s, include the institution and when you graduated. (If you are a high school graduate, don't mention that unless you went to the School of Performing Arts or some other impressive secondary institution.)

(b) Do say *where* you were born, combined with other data. Don't say *when* you were born. It doesn't matter and sometimes could be a negative — you're too young, too old, too middle-aged in someone's eyes...until they buy your book, and then it doesn't matter.

(c) Mention your marital status briefly, and any children you may have, but don't make a big deal out of it. "John Alden is married and lives with his wife, Priscilla, and their two daughters in San Francisco, California." Nobody cares about the ages of your children and their names, trust me on this one. Even if you're writing a parenting book, a mention of your parental status in the main text is sufficient. "As a parent of three sons, I..." Don't tell the editor how smart or attractive your spouse is. You're supposed to think that. The rest of us don't care.

If you are not married, you can mention it or not. Same with divorced. I think I'd avoid using the word "separated" because that sounds rather inconclusive.

(d) It's certainly not required, but if you can think of any personality traits or skills that sound good, include them briefly here. For example, I invariably include the fact that I meet deadlines.

Do *not* say this if you have a deadline problem! I also say that I am an excellent researcher and interviewer. If you can't think of any relevant skills or features, that is okay. But do try. Here are some examples of positive traits that might apply to you:

- Persistent

- Thorough

- Excellent (or at least, good) researcher

- Ability to make difficult topics understandable

- Tenacious in getting important facts

How long should the About the Author section be? No more than a page and a half, max. You're wonderful, it's true. But that's enough room to show how and why.

Should you attach your resume? You can but I tend to believe that a narrative description of your background is better. If the editor wants your resume too, he or she will ask for it.

4.2.e Specifications

In the specifications section you should briefly state how long it will take you to write the book and how many words you are offering. Most authors set a timeline of about four to six months for completion. (If an editor wants it faster, he or she will tell you.) As for word count, allow about 250 words per page of manuscript. An average book manuscript is about 70,000 words (around 280 pages), although they may be shorter or longer. Use your best guesstimate as to how long your book will be.

4.2.f The outline

The outline is an important part of your proposal because it shows what information you will include in each chapter. I generally go with no more than 20 chapters. Each chapter must have a subject and should be broken down into subsections with subheads. You can use sentence fragments — in fact, that is preferable. Most outlines are around three or four pages long, though they can be a few pages longer.

Sample 2 shows the basic format for an outline. Remember that most books have at least ten chapters. This sample shows only the first two chapters. (I am being silly with my topic in the sample, but I think silliness can be a good teaching tool.)

Basic Format For a Book Outline

Outline for MEN FROM MARS

I. Chapter One: How We Know Martians Are Here

    A. The Venusians Told Us

    B. The Proof Is in the *National Enquirer*

    C. First-Person Accounts

    D. Other Evidence

II. Chapter Two: Are Their Intentions Good or Evil? How We Know

    A. Their First Contact Behavior

    B. Current Martian-Human Relations

    C. Reversal of Global Warming Since Their Arrival

4.2.g Sample chapters

Most people include the first and sometimes the second chapter in their book proposal, although there is no rule that you must send chapter 1. Make sure you send a good chapter that holds the reader's attention and delivers on what you promise. Count on this one fact: anyone interested in your proposal will read your sample chapter or chapters very carefully. So don't scrimp on time or attention to this important part of your proposal.

The sample chapter should be at least 30 pages long — a little longer is okay. You can include simple illustrations if you want, but don't clutter up your copy. The text is what the editor is interested in, in most cases. So forget the graphics. You can allude to any fancy graphics or photographs that you plan to include in a special section of your proposal.

4.2.h Other basics

Should you have a Table of Contents for your proposal? Some people do and some don't. But you should definitely adhere to the following guidelines:

- Double-space your pages.

- Check for spelling or grammar errors. You don't want some minor mistake to derail your chances.

- Be neat. Pages should not be replete with erasures. Most writers compose with a word-processing program.

- Use white paper. Rarely (if ever) will colorful paper make someone decide they must publish your book.

- Include your name and address. Certainly in your query letter you must include that information. But include it in the proposal body as well, unless your agent tells you that you should not.

4.3 When should you send out your query and proposal?

I recommend that you finish writing your proposal before you send out any query letters to editors or agents. What if they love your letter and want to see the proposal right away? If it's already written, you can send it out immediately. If not, you are in a time crunch.

The query letter is similar to the letter you write to pitch a magazine article (see Samples 3 and 4 in chapter 7). Your first paragraph includes an interesting (brief) anecdote, fact, or quotation. Then you say that you plan to write a book on X and explain (briefly) why you think you're the right person to write this book — because of your academic credentials, personal experience, or special knowledge.

You end the one-page letter by asking the editor if he or she would like to see your proposal. If an editor then calls you or writes to you and indicates that he or she does wish to see the proposal, you send it right out. Send by regular mail. Overnight doesn't impress anybody anymore.

5. The offer

Here's what most people do when they receive their first book offer: no matter what the terms and conditions or the amount of the advance, they are so euphoric that they immediately accept without a nano-second's delay.

Do not do this! At least sleep on the decision. The editor is not going to snatch the offer away in 24 hours.

How do you evaluate an offer? You look at the amount of advance and you also look at the royalty percentage. If the advance is low (below $2,000 or zero), then look at whether the royalty percentage is at least 10%. A rule of thumb that most authors with a few books under their belt follow is this: get as much money as you can up front. With luck, your book will be successful and the royalties will flow and flow. But sadly, this does not always happen. Thus, if you have the advance, that's hard money. If the book does well, you get more. If the book doesn't do well, you don't have to give back the advance.

One tactic that you might try, although most writers are too timorous, is to ask for more than what they offer. If they offer you $3,000, ask if you could get $4,000. If they offer you $5,000, ask for $6,000. If they offer you $10,000, ask for $12,000. The answer might well be no. It could also be yes. And if it is no, you can generally default to the lower offer. When the editor makes you an offer, no contracts are drawn up until you have received and accepted the offer. This gives you time to negotiate the best possible terms.

6. Fiction

Although fiction is not my forte, many writers do well writing fiction exclusively or by switching back and forth from fiction to nonfiction. Keep in mind that writing nonfiction involves more than just reporting dull, dry facts. You should also use imagery, descriptions, and fiction-writing techniques in nonfiction.

As with nonfiction works, fiction writers must keep readers in mind when querying a potential market. You should not submit a novel about a virginal and ethereal young girl to a publisher that is noted for torrid and explicit romances.

So how do you know what they want? Read novels and contact the publishers of novels you like. Ask for writer's guidelines. Sometimes an author will thank his or her editor in the acknowledgments of a book. You can direct your query letter to that person. (Call the publishing house first to verify that the editor is still there.)

If an editor is tentatively interested in the idea you describe in your query letter, he or she will ask you to submit more, usually a synopsis of the novel and a description of the characters. The editor may then want to see several chapters or perhaps the entire manuscript.

7. Coauthoring

What about writing a book with another person? There are many reasons why two or more people might write a book together. Often each person has special knowledge or expertise, so together they can perform an excellent job. In other cases, one author has special credentials, such as a medical degree or doctorate, thus lending credibility to the book, while the second author is the person who actually writes the book.

7.1 Pros and cons of coauthorship

As a person who has coauthored books with several people, I can tell you that it can be a wonderful experience or a horrible nightmare. I've had both experiences.

It is wonderful if you are working with a coauthor who understands what he or she is expected to do and who agrees to do it. This person has a positive and helpful attitude. It is a horrible nightmare if your coauthor agrees to work with you and then refuses to do any research, lies about completed deadlines, and, worst of all, complains about *you*, the person doing all the work, to the editor. I guess the best defense really is an offense for some people.

Don't assume that you'll automatically have a good coauthoring experience with a friend you've known for 20 years. When it comes to working together on a book, people can become very territorial.

So how do you protect yourself? As much as possible, get to know your prospective coauthor. Ask yourself these questions:

- Does he or she have strong enthusiasm for the project?
- Does he or she have the time to perform this job?

If you are coauthoring with three or more authors, one person should be designated as the editor of the project.

- Does he or she have a generally positive outlook?

- Has he or she coauthored a book before? If so, get the name of the coauthor and call that person. If you're going to get any information out of the former coauthor (and you may not), it will come out in a flood, like water out of a dam with a hole blown into it.

7.2 Write a contract first

If you feel that this coauthorship can work, then make sure that you and your coauthor have signed a contract outlining the project. Some organizations such as the American Society of Journalists & Authors provide sample agreements to members. Any contract should stipulate the following items:

- Who will be in charge of the project? One person has to be the project manager. It isn't necessarily the person with the credentials; often it is the freelance writer.

- Who will do the research for the project?

- What will each person be responsible for? This can cover the overall writing style, the accuracy of content, and any other areas that are important.

- How will you split the advance? Will you split it up 50/50? If you do, will the person who does the lion's share of the work resent this?

- Describe the timing of the collaboration: who will do what and by when?

- If there is a dispute, how will you resolve it?

Even a good contract cannot ensure that you will have an idyllic relationship. But the more you consider the issues and potential problems ahead of time, and try to account for them in a contract, the better off you will be.

Be sure to look at the section on ghostwriting in chapter 3 for more tips on what to think about before agreeing to coauthor a book.

8. Magazines or books?

Which is better: writing for magazines or writing books? Writers constantly debate this question. The crux of the argument is which pays best and which works best *for you*.

Whether you are writing for magazines, book publishers, corporate clients, or individuals, what pays best depends on your talents, negotiating skills, and ability to get jobs. These areas are covered in the next few chapters, where I discuss getting assignments, marketing yourself, and working with editors and other clients.

CHAPTER 6

Getting Assignments

You've imbued yourself with the necessary writer's mindset, you've pondered the differences between writing books and writing for magazines, newspapers, corporate clients, and individuals, and you're ready to start your writing career. But how do you get ideas for topics to write about? And how do you get assignments once you find great ideas?

In this chapter I discuss generating ideas and finding places where you can sell them.

1. Finding ideas to write about

There are so many things to write about if you only take the time to consider the possibilities. Ideas can pop up at any time or place, including during the following activities.

1.1 Reading

Writers love to read. You need not concentrate on only culturally enlightening material — reading the latest bestsellers keeps you in tune with current language use and popular style. And it's fun too!

Read writers' magazines and newsletters. I have gained many leads from *Freelance Writer's Report*, a newsletter published by Cassell Communications in North Stratford, New Hampshire.

If you're interested in both fiction and nonfiction writing, also read *Writer's Digest*. If you prefer to write fiction, *The Writer* is a good monthly source of markets. (See the Appendix for addresses.) When you learn about a new market, it might suggest a story idea to you.

Check local newspapers. Perhaps a local club is running a special contest or a local resident has won recognition for a unique accomplishment. If this is something that has national appeal, consider writing a story on it for a national publication — or for a national club's publication. Would it interest businesspeople? Hobbyists? Other markets?

Many writers say that one lifetime is not long enough to explore every subject that interests them.

1.2 Listening

Listen to your friends, relatives, and colleagues. What are they worried and concerned about? I wrote my first feature article back in 1981. At the time I lived in New Hampshire, which was about to be infested by the gypsy moth caterpillar. People were extremely upset about the impending tree holocaust. I knew this from listening to people at the post office or supermarket and from talking to my friends.

My query for an article about the gypsy moth caterpillar was accepted almost instantly. The article was published, and although I resolved never to do another insect article, I added a very good clip to my file.

1.3 Looking at your own life

After adopting a child, I wrote several books on adoption, most recently *Adoption Options Complete Handbook* for Americans and Canadians interested in detailed information about agencies and support groups. I wrote *How to Live with a Mentally Ill Person* after my daughter achieved a significant and almost miraculous recovery from schizophrenia. I have also written about Attention Deficit Disorder and other problems experienced within my own family, as well as many self-help or informative articles based on personal experiences. If it happened to you and you resolved a problem, you have the potential to help others — and get paid!

1.4 Watching a little television

This recommendation may sound heretical to many writers. Television may well be a "vast wasteland," but there are many ideas that you can gain by watching (a limited amount of) television. Watch the "talking heads" and watch the news for ideas on what are current issues.

1.5 Getting out of the house

Join clubs, meet people, and network. The more you interact with others, the more you learn and the more ideas you can generate for possible writing assignments. In fact, you may write about some of the people you meet. Or they may hire you to write articles or reports for them.

1.6 Attending conferences

Go to writers' conferences when you can, particularly if the featured speakers are publishers, editors, or agents from New York or other big cities. Local conferences can also be fun, but if you can afford it, splurge on the conference in a city several hours away or even in another area. This gives you a chance to mix and mingle with potential customers from geographically diverse areas. You never know what ideas they might give you — or what jobs they might assign you when they hear where you are from.

I was approached by an editor at a conference and asked if I could write an encyclopedia on adoption and come up with at least 100 different topics. By our breakfast meeting the next day I had my list of 100+ topics ready. *The Encyclopedia of Adoption* was published in 1991, and I have updated the book for the year 2000. (Unlike people, books can have more than one life. One of my books went through three radical revisions and is still in print.) This is an example of effective networking, a skill you must cultivate.

Sometimes individuals who attend conferences are actively seeking writers. A colleague of mine was approached by a woman who was seeking a ghostwriter to write her life story. The two struck a deal at the conference.

Of course, writers' conferences don't always generate book or magazine assignments, but they usually offer sources of helpful information as well as tremendous enthusiasm for the writing field. Since most writers work alone, talking to others in the same field can be fulfilling and encouraging.

At some seminars, writers have the opportunity to sign up for one-on-one sessions with agents or editors during the conference. If you attend an event that offers such a session, sign up and come prepared with several well-thought-out ideas.

1.7 Networking

Although your fellow writers are also potential competitors, they may have opportunities they can share or jobs they don't want or don't need.

When you are offered a job that isn't suitable or doesn't interest you, why not offer it to a fellow writer? I have done this, and payback time may eventually come around when your fellow writer offers you a chance at an interesting job — although I don't think you should keep a really tight scorecard in your head.

It may be hard to network with fellow writers because many are rather individualistic. But you can meet other writers at clubs or in on-line computer forums, such as the Journalism Forum (JForum) or Literary Forum (LitForum) on CompuServe. Also check out the listserv newsletters for writers in the Appendix.

1.8 Brainstorming

Use brainstorming to come up with good ideas. Make a list of what you are knowledgeable and curious about and see if there are any crossovers. Spinning off ideas and categories of ideas is a good way to maximize your writing revenues. Write down all your ideas, even the ones that seem silly. They may not be that silly or they may springboard you to think of a truly excellent idea.

2. Break down your ideas into their elements

What do you do with an idea when you have it? How do you know what market it is for? How do you know what slant to put on the article you write? To find the proper niche for an idea, consider all its possible elements before you pitch it to any particular magazine. Ask yourself the following questions about your idea:

- Gender: Is this an idea that would appeal more to women or men?

- Age: What age bracket would be most intrigued by this idea?

- Geography: Is this idea of national interest or is it more likely to be of regional or local importance?

- Ethnic background: Are readers likely to be white, black, Native American, Hispanic, or members of another specific ethnic group?

- Genre: Is this idea more amenable to a self-help/how-to article or book or would it fit better as an op-ed piece, biography, or another genre?

- Is this idea best for a general interest market or a trade market? ("Trade" refers to a specific group, such as the septic tank sellers of Canada or the tree lovers of Washington. I don't know if there are publications for these groups, but it would not surprise me to learn that there are.)

If your idea centers on a particular person, you may find that he or she could fit in many different markets. You can ask yourself the same questions I've just listed for any ideas. In addition, list the elements that make up the person you're writing about by finding out the following information:

- Does the person belong to any special clubs or fraternal organizations? (Clubs often have magazines.)

- Is the person religious? (Religious magazines often publish profiles.)

- Is or was the person in military service? (Aim for military publications.)

- Does the person have any hobbies? (There are magazines for people who collect toy trains, Beanie babies, stamps...you name it!)

- Does the person hold an office in any organization — or did he or she hold office within the past ten years? (The organization may have a publication.)

I'm sure you can come up with other personal elements, but these are provided to get you started.

3. Fitting ideas into niches

Once you've broken your story idea into its elements, look at potential markets and determine what focus you should put on the story for each publication.

For example, I interviewed senior citizens in Florida who were helping the police by analyzing patterns of crime statistics. I wrote about them for a national retirement magazine, a Florida retirement magazine, a police magazine, and a retired officer magazine. (Two of the men I interviewed were retired from the military service.)

Each article was unique, slanted or targeted to the readers of that particular publication. Yet my basic research covered me for all of them; the only extra work I had to do was make one or two quick calls to add a little extra information.

In another case, I wrote about a woman who sold teddy bears through the mail. I wrote about her for an entrepreneurial magazine, a Boston business publication, a woman's publication, and a teddy bear trade magazine. I could have continued writing about her, but other topics captured my attention.

These examples show how you can optimize your research and time by using what you've already learned and building on that knowledge for future projects.

3.1 Do you need to specialize?

Does this mean you must specialize in one topic and work on it until the day you decide to retire or quit writing? Some people specialize in one area, but find many different niches within their specialty. For example, they may write only travel articles but consider themselves "generalists" because they write travel pieces for many different markets. Or perhaps they write health care articles, but write them for both consumer and trade markets.

Then there are others, like me, who write about many different topics in totally unrelated fields. But I can build on what I have already learned in other markets, and so can you. After all, many great discoveries have been made by people not in the field. New entrants to a field bring fresh eyes and fresh perspectives.

Sometimes you can resell an article you have written with no changes at all, which is nice. If you have sold one-time or first rights only to a publication, then you have the right to turn around and sell your article to another company after your article is published. The checks aren't usually huge — but it's nice to receive $50 or $100 for virtually no effort or expense, other than the letter I sent. I usually photocopy the entire piece so that it is very obvious to the prospective client that it has already been published.

3.2 Resell your articles — or use articles to sell yourself

You may be able to resell your article — rewritten or sometimes as a reprint — to many different markets and get a good return on the time and money you've expended.

You may also be able to use your clips from one job to win a job in a related field, even if you know nothing about it. The editor or prospective client takes the level of research and the quotations you have used carefully into account. I recommend sending a variety of samples to show your diversity.

For example, I used a lengthy report I wrote on "repetitive strain injuries" to obtain contracts for writing about health care topics. The editors presumed I had some basic knowledge as well as the capacity to learn because they had spoken to me on the telephone and they had reviewed my clips. I have also written about the business end of health care, based on the fact that I have many business clips and have earned an MBA.

4. Studying publications you want to write for

If you have an idea that you think would fit a particular magazine, read through at least one copy of the publication to see if you're on target. Sometimes the title of the magazine may sound very different from the actual subject matter, and editors consistently report that their pet peeve is being queried with off-the-wall ideas that don't begin to fill their needs. Don't make this mistake!

Before you send out query letters or manuscripts, understand who it is you are writing to and why this editor or publisher or client may be interested in your idea. Dana Cassell, publisher of *Freelance Writer's Report*, says, "Many writers have an idea and think that everybody wants to know about it, so they shotgun it out there. But different magazines have different readers and different demographics."

As you read a magazine, look at the content and style of the articles. Ask yourself the following questions as part of your analysis:

- Do the writers use a lot of quotations?

- Are the articles heavily anecdotal?

- What kind of advertisements are included and what kind of people would they appeal to most?

- If there is a "Letters to the Editor" section, what are readers concerned about?

- Do articles seem heavily researched, with many charts, graphs, and numerical references?

- Who are the authors of the articles? Read the short author bios if they are included at the end of an article or elsewhere in the magazine. Are most writers people with specific credentials, such as an M.D. or Ph.D.? If so, your idea might be wonderful but it could be turned down if you are not a doctor.

- Are articles heavily illustrated with graphics or are they dominated by text?

If a periodical is full of ads to help you stay younger, rid your face of wrinkles, and help you exercise, and there's little mention of children or parenting, it would probably not be a good idea to suggest a be-a-better-parent article to the editor.

On the other hand, if the magazine is full of ads for baby products, your idea on how to cope with the all-night new-baby blues could be of interest.

Don't limit yourself to the questions I've listed here. Think of some of your own and add to the list. Look at the column written by the editor or publisher, if there is one. Often he or she highlights key areas of concern and this section is important because it may generate ideas.

Incidentally, you don't have to order or buy all the magazines you may wish to write for. Every time I visit the doctor or dentist, I quickly thumb through every magazine in the office. If my name is called before I'm finished perusing a publication, I ask permission to borrow it. No one has denied permission so far. And yes, I have found markets for my work from this exercise.

Don't send your article on illicit sex to a religious publication and don't send a clip about the power of prayer to a men's publication that you want to write for. Instead, gauge what you send to what you think your potential customer wants.

CHAPTER 7

Marketing: A Key to Success

You have a great book contract or maybe six magazine articles lined up — or both! You're on your way and won't have to worry anymore about getting jobs, right?

Wrong! The successful writer never forgets the importance of marketing, which refers to actively selling your ideas to prospective clients. Editors leave, magazines fail, and publishing houses are sold, merged, or folded. Businesspeople retire and clients move on. Because of this, it is wise to spend at least 20% to 30% of your time working on obtaining more work — from your old customers as well as new ones.

Yet when you have plenty of work to do, it is natural to concentrate on doing that work and to forget about next month or next year. Don't make this mistake.

You should always be sending out query letters, updating your resume and Web site, and letting individuals, publishers, and businesses know that you are available to do any writing jobs that they need. In this chapter I will suggest ways to keep your name and talents in the forefront of potential clients' minds.

> Marketing is important because you never win all the jobs you bid on. No matter how a client may rave about your work, he or she may be unable or unwilling to hire you.

1. Keep those query letters coming

You write a query letter to convince an editor to hire you to write a book or article. If it is a query for a magazine article, you either get the go-ahead or a rejection, although sometimes the editor requests more information. If the query relates to a book, its purpose is to intrigue an editor sufficiently so that he or she will ask to look at a complete proposal (see chapter 5). Samples 3 and 4 show query letters for a profile and a business article.

Sometimes you get no reply at all. Follow up after a month or so if you still want to do the piece.

I have had editors contact me over a year after I submitted queries to them! One told me he found my query after he moved the file cabinet and asked if I still wanted to write the book. In that case, I did not.

The following are some basic elements that you should be sure to incorporate into your one-page, single-spaced letter:

- Start with a fact, anecdote, or interesting statistic. It should be something that will capture the reader's interest and inspire him or her to read on.

- Explain in one or two paragraphs what you want to write about and why readers of this publication would be interested.

- Give your slant or hook. The slant is the underlying angle or thesis of your article. For example, is the sea life in your area being killed or injured by boaters? Is the recent layoff at a large plant going to drastically affect the local economy? Or perhaps your slant is one of national scope. For example, you see a trend toward older Americans returning to work. Sell the angle that you'd like to pursue.

- Identify yourself in the second or third paragraph, including why you are the right person for this job and any special credentials you may have. (If you don't have any special credentials, don't worry about it. But don't mention that you lack them, as some novice writers do.)

Sample Query Letter For a Profile

July 29, 200-

Mary Alice Teddy
Teddies Forever
999 Maple Lane Road
Wonderful, NJ 00000

Dear Ms. Teddy:

Most people have books on their bookshelves, but Fran Lewis has collectible teddy bears on display in her living room bookcase. She has bears sitting in the living room, bears in the bedrooms, and bears in the bathroom.

Lewis is known as the "Bear Lady" in Concord, Massachusetts. Not only does she love bears, but she also sells them to fellow bear lovers worldwide. She has even hired bear designers to create unique bears for her mail-order catalogue.

I'm a freelance writer with many credits for writing profiles. (Several of my clips are enclosed.) I'd like to write a profile of Lewis, the Bear Lady, for your publication; I'm offering 1,500 words. My slant will be how bears dominate Lewis's business and personal life.

Thank you.
Christine Adamec

Sample Query Letter For a
Business Periodical

July 29, 200—

Ms. Sally Nofrills
Business Only
5555 Elm Tree Lane
Toronto, ON   Z1P OG6

Dear Ms. Nofrills:

Fran Lewis will earn just under $1 million this year selling teddy bears by mail. Sound frivolous? She's a tough businesswoman who wouldn't end her business when her husband walked out, her partner quit, and the bank called in her loan.

"I never give up," she said. And she doesn't.

Today, Lewis sells a variety of teddy bears to adult collectors throughout the United States, both by catalogue and in her retail business. She plans to expand the business as well, taking on additional staff and products.

I'm a business writer who would like to write a business profile for you on Lewis, the "Bear Lady" of Concord, Massachusetts. I've written numerous business pieces in the past and several clips are enclosed. I have an MBA and I meet deadlines.

Does 2,000 words plus photos sound like it might fit your needs?

Thank you.

Christine Adamec

- State how many words you are proposing to write and roughly when you can deliver the piece. There are about 250 words on a double-spaced typewritten page. If the word count you offer is too much or too little, the editor can tell you how much to write if he or she wants the piece.

- If you have been published before, tell the editor you'd be happy to forward clippings if he or she is interested. If you don't have any clips, do not say you are a novice writer.

1.1 To SASE or not to SASE? That is the question

Many new writers agonize over whether or not they should send a SASE (self-addressed stamped envelope). Many writers' publications routinely advise new writers to enclose a SASE with their query letters.

I violate this "rule" constantly. I believe that if an editor is interested enough in my idea, he or she will spend the postage to tell me so, or pick up the telephone or send me an e-mail. And if the editor doesn't like the idea, I'll probably receive a form letter or short note. My attitude is, why should I pay to receive a rejection letter?

If you must send a SASE, don't provide enough postage to send your clips or other material back. They will never look as good as when you sent them. I have clean copies to send out with my next query letter. Nor do I need to have my resume returned. I have the file on disk and can produce a beautiful clean copy anytime I want to.

That said, I know that many people still think it's mandatory to enclose a SASE. If you do send a SASE with your letter, I recommend that you send only your query and not a ream of clips to go with it. Imagine how much postage that will cost to return! Instead, tell the editor that you will provide samples of your writing if needed. If you don't have any samples, say nothing.

1.2 Shrinking violets don't get assignments

Another point to bear in mind as you write your query letter is that you must sell yourself. I recommend you abandon modesty about your abilities and your accomplishments. (Don't be arrogant, of course, and never lie!)

If you don't have any writing credits or any credits in the area you're querying about, do not say so. It's a major mistake to refer to what you don't have. Instead, allude to your positive attributes or accomplishments that relate to the story you want to write. For example, let's say that you're an active environmentalist and won a "green" award last year. This is proof that you're just the right author for that recycling piece. Or say you've written over 20 personality profiles on businesspeople, and thus you're perfect to profile a celebrity for a popular magazine.

Be sure to refer to personal strengths. For example, I make it a point to tell every editor that I meet deadlines. (If I am going to be late, I make a point to notify the editor I'm working for.) Or perhaps you are an excellent and rapid researcher.

Whenever possible, tie in your personal strengths with the needs of the publication. For example, you may be an expert skateboarder, but that is irrelevant if you want to sell an article on some early childhood development issue (unless it has to do with skateboarding!).

1.3 Should you include your resume too?

Some writers include their resume in all query letters. I keep one on file, but I am rarely asked for it. Instead, I am asked for samples of my work. If the client likes my work and wants to hire me, he or she doesn't care about my academic credentials or what I did right after graduating from college.

1.4 Keep copies of your query letters!

Be sure to make a copy of your query. It is embarrassing if an editor calls and asks you to write an article you forgot that you had queried about. (This is the voice of experience: it happened to me once a very long time ago. I never made that mistake again.) Keep a printed out copy of your query and also keep the query on disk so that you have a backup.

1.5 Move right on

After you send out your query, start working on your next one. Do not sit and wait to receive an assignment. You should have at least three to four queries (preferably more) out at any one time in order to maintain a steady workflow. Inevitably, some of your great ideas will be rejected, but when you still have several ideas out there, a rejection is much less painful.

> Try to write compelling query letters, and let your enthusiasm shine through.

2. Telephone queries

Some writers believe that calling up an editor, publisher, or other person to pitch an idea is the height of tackiness. I disagree. You may have a wonderful idea that is very timely and you don't want to wait to convey your idea to the person who needs it.

If you're going to talk to someone you already know, your telephone query should be relatively easy. Be sure you've got your basic idea clearly in your mind, and be prepared to talk about your slant, when you can have the article done, how long you think it will be, etc.

If you are calling a total stranger — a "cold call" — write down a few notes ahead of time. Psyche yourself up, put on your best "smiley face" voice, and think of yourself as a runner crashing through the tape at the finish line.

> You could fax your urgent queries, but unsolicited faxes annoy many people. I recommend using the telephone.

When you call, be certain to ask if it is a convenient time to talk. The editor may be rushing to meet a deadline or puzzling over some confusing data. If he or she says it is not a good time, ask if you may call back. In most cases, the answer is yes.

I like telephone queries because when the editor expresses reservations or concerns about my topic, I can counteract them immediately. For example, perhaps the editor is worried that the subject won't appeal to baby boomers. If this is unfounded, you can point out that baby boomers are concerned about this topic and provide some evidence.

One thing to keep in mind is that the more the other person talks and the more you listen, the more likely it is that you'll make a sale. This technique works far better than the talk-only mode employed by too many people who sell products. The editor or publisher wants to know that his or her special needs are being taken into account. Listen carefully to find out what those needs are. If you are too busy talking about your own goals and expect the editor to listen to you, he or she will quickly tune you out.

Most people are used to others *not* listening to them. People truly wish to be heard and if you are one of those rare people who can listen and also respond, then you will be considered a valuable asset.

Sometimes when you make a telephone or written query, the editor may not be interested in the idea you're pitching, but he or she may have a different and perhaps even more compelling idea he or she would like to offer you as an assignment. Listen and consider the offer. It could be your opportunity to break into this market.

However, don't say yes right away, no matter how much you want to. Find out what the alternative idea is and think about whether you would like to do it or not. Editors don't give the easy assignments to unknown writers — you're more likely to get a tough job that the editor doesn't have time to do or doesn't know how to do, or both.

Other times the editor may say that he or she does not want your article immediately, but that the topic might be more relevant in a few months. Ask if you can call back then.

Realize that editors work well ahead of schedule. Your wonderful article about Christmas should not be submitted in October or November. Think "Christmas in July" and submit it then. Never underestimate the importance of good timing.

3. Online marketing

One fairly new method of marketing yourself and landing assignments is through computer networks such as America Online or by directly contacting someone via an e-mail address you find on a Web site. (Be sure to read chapter 12 on the Internet.)

There is a certain camaraderie to online networks, and querying via e-mail can be less formal than querying by mail or even by a cold call. This does not, however, mean there are never any problems with online assignments.

As with all your jobs, you should be careful. Ask questions. Certainly you should always ask for a significant up-front payment: at least one third of the entire job.

On the other hand, if you are careful and keep your eyes open, you can spot many good opportunities. I wrote profiles for a trade magazine for several years, starting when a new publisher left word on CompuServe that he was looking for a business writer.

3.1 E-mail queries

I don't use e-mail queries much, but once in awhile, if I think I have a great idea, I will send an electronic message to an editor. I keep it short, explaining what the idea is, why I think it will sell, and why I want this particular publisher to buy it. I then expect either no response or many questions before a deal is cut. I have sold two books through e-mail queries.

3.2 Personal Web site

I don't use a personal Web site either, though I am listed on some writing Web sites and at my agent's site. If you have the ability to put together a Web site advertising your writing business, it's probably worth doing. This is undoubtedly an approach that will become more common in the next couple of years.

4. Self-publishing

If you choose to do your own publishing, whether it's a newsletter, a booklet, or a book, you need to market the product. In fact, the time to start selling is before your newsletter or book is launched, so you can raise some capital to get it going.

I have published a monthly newsletter on adoption, selling it to a very specialized market made up primarily of adoption agencies. (I am in the process of selling this newsletter now because other projects require more of my time.) I built up my list of customers from responses to direct-mail postcards that I sent to potential readers. I reviewed magazines such as *Adoptive Families* for ads from organizations and individuals whose addresses were published and who might be interested in my newsletter. In addition, I actively solicited names from contacts in the field, people I had discovered when I researched my book on adoption.

If an individual is launching a new magazine and wants to pay you later, shy away. Later may never come — the magazine may fold before he or she pays you.

It is also possible to buy mailing lists for relatively low fees. I bought lists from several specialized sources — for example, adoption agencies; the newsletter *The Adopted Child*; the National Adoption Information Clearinghouse in Rockville, Maryland; and also advertised in Tapestry Books, a company that concentrates on selling adoption books by many different publishers, in Ringoes, New Jersey.

5. Vanity presses

A vanity press is a publisher that will publish your book for a fee. Be careful of vanity presses that make grandiose promises; they usually can't and don't deliver. They make their money from your money, rather than by selling your book. If your book sells any copies at all, they are most likely to be copies that you sell.

Sometimes a vanity publisher will work out well for you. For example, let's say you're a businessperson who needs a brochure or pamphlet and you need minor editing. There are legitimate enterprises that can take your project from a rough draft to a final product. Always be cautious, however; it is your money.

CHAPTER 8

Communicating With Editors and Clients

Once you have your idea and have sold it to an editor, or sold your services to an individual or business, you may think it's smooth sailing from here on: all you have to do is finish writing your assignment and collect a check.

It may be that easy, but it may not be too. You may have to learn how to work with a particular editor. Or your customers may have little or no experience working with freelance writers and will not know how to deal with you. You need to educate them, and this chapter offers advice on the care and training of your clients.

Sometimes relationships break down and you may no longer get along with an editor or customer. This chapter also covers what to do when that happens.

What editors care about

Most editors, like most workers everywhere, want to do a good job, receive praise at least once in a while, and, if possible, get promoted. If an editor thinks your well-written pieces can further these goals, then that editor will value you highly.

Of course, editors have other goals as well. They want to satisfy their readers. Whether they admit it or not, advertisers are important, too, if the publication is one that accepts ads.

Editors want solidly backed facts and information with quotations that were actually said by the person quoted. They do not want to get sued because someone was misquoted. Few writers fake quotes, but, unfortunately, some do.

Editors also want copy that captures and holds the reader's attention all the way to the end of the piece.

1. Editors are people

Many new writers forget that editors are human too. They have the power to accept or reject your work, hence they may seem godlike. But they also get stomachaches sometimes, and they have mortgages, kids, and problems. They have their ups and downs just like everyone else. So how do you deal with editors as professionals, yet still allow them to be people too?

(a) *Don't call an editor just to chat.* Be friendly, but be sure each call has a purpose. If you have a hot idea or an important point to make, use the telephone, but keep it brief. If it's not urgent, send a letter, fax, or e-mail message. Be pleasant, but professional.

(b) *Avoid calling editors on Monday mornings before 10:00 a.m. their time.* Always check the telephone directory to see what time zone the editor is in. Many people have the Monday morning blahs, or a staff meeting, or an overstuffed in-basket awaiting them at work. They may not be very responsive.

(c) *Also avoid calling on Friday afternoon.* This is when people are frantically trying to wrap up their work, and they don't want any diversions. The day before or after a holiday weekend is another time to avoid, especially in late December.

(d) *Always ask the editor if this is a convenient time to call.* If it's not, offer to call back.

(e) *Never expect an immediate reply from an editor to your written communications, particularly when an editor is a new client.* Some editors may take as long as four to six weeks to reply to a letter. After that time, you may follow up with a polite note or quick telephone call.

1.1 Making an editor's job easier

Although I have often joked that I don't have to worry about typographical errors because that's why God made editors, I truly believe it is important to edit your own work carefully. Even if you have a computer program that checks grammar and spelling, there are still things it won't pick up.

> Check for spelling errors and typographical errors and correct them. Do not rely on your computer's spell checker. Some serious errors can slip through when words are spelled just fine — but aren't the words you meant.

When you feel that your draft is pretty much in its final stages, whether it is a report, magazine feature, or an entire book, I recommend you read it very critically *as a reader*, not as an author.

Reread the letter or contract directing you to do the job and make sure you have included what was requested before you send it in. Put a manuscript away for a few days and then come back to it. You'll be amazed at how you will be able to see possible improvements.

Ask yourself the following questions:

- ▣ Is this interesting and will it keep my reader reading?

- ▣ Does it make sense? Are there some statements that are unsupported or not backed up that should be?

- ▣ Is it clear? Will all my readers understand it? (If you have used any technical jargon, will it be clear to anyone unfamiliar with the words?)

- ▣ Do I have a good "flow" and transition of paragraphs from one idea to another? Are there any sections that seem to "stick" and that might take the reader aback?

Read the first paragraph of an article and the last paragraph. Do they seem to have any relationship to each other whatsoever? If the project is lengthy, read the first paragraph of a chapter and the last paragraph. Or you may prefer to read the first and last pages. There should be a common thread that ties together your theme. If not, then make it so.

Read at least part of the piece aloud. When you read aloud, you can often hear problems that are not obvious when you read silently.

Perfection is not required but it is a good idea to catch as many errors as you can and get rid of them.

1.2 Get it in writing

Many new and experienced writers rely solely on telephone conversations for the terms and conditions expected by both sides. But memories fail, people become confused, and editors sometimes quit.

Clarify your terms and conditions in writing. Forego, for a moment, your ecstasy about getting the go-ahead and be sure to consider the merits of the actual offer.

If the offer is made to you verbally and the terms and conditions sound reasonable, ask the editor to send you a letter summarizing what you've discussed. Some editors use contracts, while others rely on letters of agreement. Others think a handshake or telephone conversation is just fine.

If your editor refuses or never gets around to writing you a contract or letter, one tactic is to "reverse contract" your client. This means that you summarize the terms and conditions as you understand them and write them out on your letterhead. Once you have sent this, try to receive some written acknowledgment from the editor — a note, fax, or letter — that states acceptance of your terms.

When the client does send you a contract, read it over carefully. If you don't like the terms and conditions or they seem different from what you thought you had agreed upon, you can either cross out the parts you don't like and initial them or you can request a new contract altogether. If in doubt, or if the contract reads like an insurance policy, ask a lawyer to review it if the fee is for $1,000 or more. (There is more on contracts in chapter 15.)

If the editor verbally promises you something extra that is not in the contract, be sure to get it in writing!

1.3 Do editors steal ideas?

New writers often worry unduly about whether magazine, newspaper, or book editors will steal their wonderful ideas. The truth is that it rarely happens.

If you have a great idea, send a query to a publication, and a year later see an article that is just like the article you would have written, does it mean that the editor stole your idea?

Probably not. He or she may have already had an article using your idea on file and that's why the publication turned you down. You cannot copyright ideas.

If you do feel, however, that your idea is sufficiently unique and that an editor stole your idea, you should send a strong letter of protest to the editor and to the editor's boss (usually the publisher). It is doubtful that you'll gain any monetary consideration, but writing the letter might make you feel better and will also make it less likely that the editor will steal any more ideas — if in fact yours was stolen.

1.4 Working with a first-time client

To launch a good working relationship with a client, ask him or her to send you samples of work he or she particularly likes before you start a project. If you are writing a business proposal, ask for several winning proposals on which to model yours. If the assignment is a magazine article, ask the editor to send you his or her personal favorite issues of the

Read the contract! Even major publishers can make silly typographical errors, and you don't want some future bureaucrat holding you to a mistaken date or fee.

magazine. If it's a book you are to write, find out what books the editor worked on and enjoyed. Seek out patterns and common denominators.

Don't try to clone what someone else did. If you are hired, presumably the client likes your work. However, what editors and publishers like and what other clients like is different. I write for two editors at the same company and one loves a lot of quotations while the other hates quotes and says they should only be used if absolutely necessary. The different publications they produce clearly show their personal preferences.

2. Customers who have never worked with freelance writers before

This happens more frequently than you might imagine, even with editors at established magazines or publishing houses. Editors come and go and may have relied heavily on staff writers. Now, however, many companies have downsized operations and editors have to contract out most of the copy.

Some editors are struggling with the nuances of dealing with a person who isn't on staff: that is, you. Try to make your dealings as pleasant and easy as possible, but do not let the editor (or any other customer) walk all over you.

How might an inexperienced editor take advantage of you? With constant calls and faxes, last-minute demands, and an unreasonable number of rewrites. You'll recognize it if you see it.

Stand firm. Avoid arguing but stick to the terms of your contract as much as possible. Do one rewrite (if that is what was agreed upon), not eight or ten. One or two telephone calls a day from an editor is pushing it. If he or she calls even more frequently, then there is some insecurity operating here, either with the editor personally, or with you, or both.

If you can tough it out and let the editor's confidence build up, you may want to hang on to him or her, especially if the pay is good. However, if things aren't working out soon, you should decide whether to drop the client or just grit your teeth and bear it. My personal opinion is that dropping a client is much easier on the psyche — and the teeth!

Sometimes customers have no idea how to deal with a contract writer because they never needed to hire a ghostwriter or proposal writer. Help them as much as possible and don't take advantage. Offer a fair price and stand by it.

Virtually all writers are approached at one time or another by people who want someone to write their life story, their marvelous adventure, or something they just know will make the *New York Times* bestseller list. The presumption is that you should be grateful that they're offering you this hot tip. Sometimes they are annoyed when you don't show extreme gratitude. Be polite and listen (occasionally the person may have a great story idea), but in most cases it is best to tactfully decline such offers. They are usually a waste of your time.

3. What if you don't get along with an editor or client?

Friction between writer and client happens more frequently than we'd like to think. One of the beauties of being your own boss is that you can "fire" an editor who you just can't work with.

Before taking that step, try to find out what's wrong. Take the direct approach and ask if there's a problem and if so, what it is. Some people have very controlling personalities and don't mean to patronize or "talk down" to others — it's just the way they are. If you find a client to be impossible, you may wish to finish the job and then never work with that person again.

Sometimes (not often) a relationship with a client can become unworkable and you find you cannot finish the job. If you are unhappy, the client probably is not happy either, and you may be able to reach an agreement on what final things you can do short of abandoning the job. (Be sure to get such an agreement in writing.)

If you disagree with the direction a client wants a piece to go, you can put up with the decision or you can argue. Do remember, however, that the customer holds the veto on editorial decisions. Always follow the "business golden rule": the person who has the gold gets to make the rules.

Keep in mind that most clients are normal, reasonable, intelligent beings, just like you.

Writers deal with many kinds of clients besides editors and publishers. Your clients may span all walks of life and many occupations.

I once dealt with an editor who seemed to want to argue about everything, no matter how trivial. Argue, argue, argue. Trying to please him was impossible. What worked? Arguing back, telling him he was wrong, and not backing down. He argued less often after I did that. Apparently he appreciated people who fought back.

4. What if the editor you like quits or is reassigned?

Frequently, just when you establish a good rapport with a particular editor — you understand what the editor needs and wants and the editor is very happy with your work — that person leaves and a new editor comes in.

The new editor doesn't know you and perhaps he or she has never worked with a freelance writer before. He or she doesn't return your calls or your letters, even though you are in the middle of a project.

What can you do? One tactic I have used is to come to a full stop on all work until the editor and I reach some agreement. You can't expect to have the same happy relationship you had with your former editor, but you should at least have a working relationship.

Send the editor a certified letter saying that you are stopping all work on the project until you can discuss what needs to be done and what direction should be taken.

You will probably get an anguished telephone call, especially if the editor really needs your project. And if you don't hear anything for awhile, don't waste your time working on a project that may ultimately be rejected.

Surprisingly, what often happens is that a good working relationship evolves between you and the new person — one that works so well that when the new editor leaves, you will feel sad.

5. When editors and clients call you

After an editor or customer becomes comfortable working with you, he or she may approach you with a request that you take on a particular job. The editor tells you how many words are needed, when the deadline is, how much you will be paid, and so on. All you have to do is say yes or no.

When the editor asks if you want to do the job, say, "Well, let me check my schedule. Um, I *think* so."

If he or she asks if the amount is enough, never say, "Gosh, I'd do that for free." Be cool. Instead say, "Well, I guess that's fair. But does that include expenses?"

Once an editor trusts you and realizes that you do good work, there's a good chance he or she will call you when something is needed in a hurry. The easy stuff, which can be given plenty of lead-time, always seems to be done in-house.

I have obtained some lucrative assignments over the Christmas holidays or in the summertime. Why? Because the client needed the job done right away and I was able to meet the deadline.

When an editor or other client is in this kind of panic situation, he or she will seek out writers through networking, computer bulletin boards, old query letters, and every possible source.

Before agreeing to such a project, you should definitely find out what the "real" deadline is. Clients will often give you a deadline that is sooner than when they need to receive the material because they are used to writers turning in their copy late, or because they want to have a comfortable chunk of time for editing.

When the client is in a big hurry, however, he or she is much more likely to give you the real deadline. If you can't churn out good copy when the client needs it, turn the job down.

Ask for money up front. Ask for half and settle for about a third. People in dire straits are more likely to agree to pay in advance. Remember that you are going to be working when other people are partying, and you may be taking a risk if you are doing this job for a new client, so factor all this into your price. (You can go out and celebrate when the check arrives.)

CHAPTER 9

Problem Situations and Common Mistakes

No matter how effective a writer and businessperson you are, problems will come up. This chapter concentrates on some common problems that writers face and possible ways to resolve them.

1. Your client hates what you write

You thought the project was fine; your client does not. So what do you do? I offer every client one free rewrite. But before I do, I need to know what the problem is.

- Does the editor want more quotes or more documentation?

- Is the article too short or too long? Maybe you've met the word count the client requested, but now he or she wants some adding or cutting.

- Is the tone wrong? Were you humorous when you should have been serious?

▣ Did you write at too high or too low a reading level?

Get as many specifics as possible from your client so that you can fix the problem.

There are those few clients who will never be satisfied, no matter what you or anyone else does. They are constantly rewriting and reorganizing and just can't let go of a project.

These editors don't usually last long because they drive their coworkers crazy. You will meet a few of them in the course of your career. If you find that you are working with such an editor, satisfy him or her as much as possible. Once the job is done, you need never work with that person again, no matter how good the money is. The emotional strain is just not worth it.

2. Sometimes you will have to miss a deadline

I have called editors from the hospital to let them know a story will be late, and why. You may not have to be quite this dramatic. But do keep editors aware if you need to be late. Remember that editors are people, and if you have a reasonable excuse for not finishing your work on time, they will usually understand.

As soon as you know that your work will probably be late, notify your client so he or she can make other arrangements. Perhaps you can have your research shipped to the client and another writer can take over the project. Or perhaps the editor can delay the project and allow you to finish it later on.

Be honest with the editor and, in most cases, he or she will be fair and honest with you.

3. A client wants to monopolize your time

This can be a nice kind of problem to have, even if it may not seem like it at the time. In some situations, clients like your work so much that they want to give you all the work they can. When you have too much work, you may have to give up other clients. Saying no is hard, especially when you have a client who likes you and pays well.

But it is important to remember that you must still spend at least 20% to 30% of your time marketing. You cannot depend on one client for all your revenues. If something should happen to that client, and things can happen very fast in the business world, you'll be out of work.

4. Some common mistakes

Probably the biggest mistake most new writers make is not realizing that writing is a business. I've spent most of this book discussing how and why you need to maintain a businesslike attitude to become a profit-making writer. Here are a few very common mistakes that both new and experienced writers tend to make.

4.1 Saying yes when you really mean no — or maybe

When your revenues are directly dependent on the work you do, it is hard to turn down a job that pays well. But sometimes you just have to say no.

You may not have the time to do this job because you have committed to other jobs. Don't sacrifice quality and your reputation by skimping on a job or shortchanging a client.

The job may be interesting but not pay enough. Or perhaps you've been writing this column for two years and don't know how to tell the editor you just can't do it anymore. Carefully determine what are your most important and lucrative jobs and how much time various jobs take.

In some cases a $200 magazine article is better than a $1,000 article for a national publication. How could this be? If the $200 article requires minimal research and takes you two hours to write, then you're earning $100 per hour. Perhaps the $1,000 article requires 60 hours or more. That means you'll earn $16.66 per hour. Sure, you'll gain prestige by having your work appear in a renowned publication. If the pay differential is worth it, then turn down the $200 job. However, be sure that you understand that more money doesn't always mean a better offer.

4.2 Agonizing over trivial details

This is a major time-waster among new writers. For example, if you sent a letter to an agent and also to a publisher about an idea you have, and if each responds and is interested, what should you do?

Unless you have a contract with the agent, you have a right to send the material to the publisher. You could send it directly to the agent and delay sending to the publisher. (Although I'd recommend the reverse. It is, after all, the publisher who is your ultimate customer.)

To avoid these dilemmas, plan ahead and set policies for yourself. Presume that everyone who receives your letter will be immediately thrilled and eager to learn more. This will help you judge whom to send queries to and how many letters to send.

4.3 Not trusting your instincts

Although I strongly believe it's important to think rationally and clearly, I also acknowledge that we all have an internal system that processes subconscious and precocious information. These are your gut feelings and it is important to listen to them.

Sometimes a project sounds perfect. The pay is generous, you like the client, his or her reputation is impeccable, and the terms and conditions of the agreement seem more than fair to you. Yet a nagging doubt persists; something in you says, "maybe not."

I'm not talking about the fear that most of us suffer at some point when we take on new challenges and do things we've never done before. Fears of inadequacy can be overcome. Instead, I'm referring to those times when there is something wrong, but you just can't pin it down. When that happens, I recommend you hold off. Delay accepting the job for at least a day or two until you can determine if it is really right for you.

4.4 Being dazzled by a high offer or a prestigious publication

When the editor or customer offers you a fee in the thousands and you've been used to receiving hundreds, it is easy to feel "blown away" and that you must accept this job.

No matter how much money you are offered, it is always important to take into account how much work this project will take. How many hours over what period of time?

Will the client expect you to dump your other customers and dedicate all your time to him or her? Is there a potential for continued work with this client or is it a one-time deal? If you do accept the job and drop all your other clients for a period of time, do you think they'll still be there waiting for you later on?

How much up-front money is involved? If the answer is zero and yet this project is a long-term one for a considerable period, then what is in it for you?

This doesn't mean that big offers must always be looked at askance or that they inevitably mean trouble. But many writers are far more likely to jump on the bandwagon and accept without thinking because they are dazzled by the dollars. Don't make that mistake.

4.5 Agreeing to work without a contract

If someone tells you that you don't really need a contract, a friendly verbal agreement is just fine, do not believe this! Politely but firmly state that you work under contracts only, whether they are a few paragraphs or 25 pages. If your prospective client still says he or she doesn't want to do a contract because there isn't time to draw one up or for some other reason, then you can create a reverse contract (see chapters 8 and 15). A reverse contract is not as good as a contract that you both sign, but if you really feel you must have this job, then at least create a reverse contract and send it by certified mail to the client. I recommend that you tell the client that you need him to sign or at least initial it.

4.6 Ignoring or rationalizing ethical dilemmas

The more successful you become, the more likely you are to encounter at least a few ethical dilemmas. You may be asked to write for clients who you don't like or who you may even consider disreputable. A client may ask you to do something that doesn't seem right to you. For example, a prospective client in another country asked me to write about American electronic firms. It sounded like industrial espionage to me and I turned it down.

Some writers write term papers and doctoral dissertations for students. I have been offered such opportunities and have turned them down. They rationalize that politicians and actors hire ghostwriters all the time. However, in my view, it is popularly known that scripts are written for politicians and actors, but when it comes to receiving a Master's degree or a Ph.D., it is assumed that the student actually did the work.

There are also lesser ethical dilemmas; for example, is it okay to share information about one editor with another? It depends. I wouldn't do it if they were direct or even indirect competitors.

If they are not competitors, sometimes you can enhance your networking by telling other editors what projects you are working on. One of my editors sent me clippings on a subject I was researching for someone else, and they turned out to be very valuable to me.

It is also a good idea, incidentally, when you receive such good cooperation from an editor to reciprocate by sending clips that might be interesting and helpful to his or her own work.

There are many possible mistakes that writers can make; I've tried to summarize the key ones. Avoid making these mistakes and instead, forge ahead and make different and less costly ones! Mistakes are unavoidable and a necessary part of learning the business. Everyone makes a few mistakes now and then.

Part 3
You've Got Assigments:
Researching the Jobs
You're Hired to Write

CHAPTER 10

Researching Basics

Once you've got assignments, whether they're for books, articles, or corporate reports, you need to do your research. Research involves finding information from magazines and books, interviewing people, and often searching databases for information. You may need to use several tactics to obtain information because what you need to know may be found in a book or a specialized database as well as in conversation with an expert.

1. Before you start to research: A few tips

1.1 Write an outline

Know what you're looking for ahead of time. Form an outline of your writing assignment either in your head or on paper.

A key fact or statistic can be the piece of the puzzle that really "makes" your case. Often a quotation from an interviewee is what your reader will walk away remembering. Never underestimate the value of good research.

After you get focused, determine what you are seeking before you enlist the aid of your librarian and other experts. Don't make busy librarians waste time helping you compile exhaustive research when all you need is general information. For instance, do you want to know about the parenting pattern of the pelican or are you just looking for general information on pelicans? How specific do you need to get? This determines the kind of reference you need. (As you learn more, you'll become more adept at picking and choosing your data.)

Your initial outline for your research is important because you need a basic idea of what you're looking for before you go out and actually find it. It's also important to keep in mind that you must be flexible; if your research reveals that you're running into a dead end, you can retreat and regroup.

For example, I was recently assigned to research how outpatient providers (primarily doctors and clinics) are reimbursed for their care of nursing home patients. I soon learned that most of the payments are government controlled. So I decided to investigate a subset of that issue — rehabilitation and physical therapy of nursing home residents when the nursing home facility directly contracts with a rehab or physical therapy provider. I would not have known about my final subject if I had not first started out with a basic plan to study nursing homes, gathered names of nursing-home administrators and organizations, and called several people to learn some basics about this subject.

The point I'm trying to get across here is that you should never just walk into a library and ask the frazzled librarian to tell you everything he or she knows about Western civilization or some other topic. Think about what you and your readers would like to know, jot down a basic outline, and revise it as you go along.

1.2 Know your audience

Keep in mind your audience and its reading level. Are your readers academics or are they people who read at the ninth grade level? If you need to keep it simple, you probably don't need to look at highly technical data, doctoral dissertations, or academic journal articles.

What questions would your readers be interested in delving into? What are their concerns and biases? As the writer/researcher, you are their representative. Put yourself in their shoes and try to imagine what they care about. People in virtually any field are intrigued by unusual topics, trends, changes in the field, and expert opinions.

1.3 Who? What? Why? Where? When? How?

Keep in mind the basics: who, what, why, where, when, and how many. For example, with regard to the pelican, how many are there, anyway? Where are they? Why are they there?

Or let's say you're writing about troubled schoolchildren. Here are some questions you might ask:

- Who are the children?

- Where are they?

- What are they doing that is bad or troubled?

- Why are they doing it?

- When are they doing it? (In school, at home, at a shopping mall — all of the above?)

- How many of them are there?

Jot down other questions you think readers would ask. You don't have to use them all, but they can spark your interest and point to details you might feature.

2. Starting your research

After you make a basic plan, what's next on the agenda? Here are a few suggestions.

2.1 Make friends with your reference librarian

Most librarians feel a special kinship with writers, so take advantage of this. The reference librarian can be the writer's best friend because he or she can help you find nearly everything ever written on your topic.

You don't have to become your librarian's soul mate. Just be nice to him or her, ask for help, and let him or her know what you're working on. Show some interest in what the library has to offer. It doesn't hurt to donate an occasional bestseller you've already read to your library. Nor does it hurt to acknowledge your librarian, in print, when your first (or subsequent) book comes out.

2.2 Learn what is available from libraries

Learn what is available in your local library as well as in libraries in neighboring cities. Virtually all libraries have copies of the *Reader's Guide to Periodical Literature*, an annual reference publication that lists each year's articles in different subject areas from a variety of periodicals. In addition, *Books in Print* is another valuable reference for finding books on a myriad of topics or authors both famous and obscure.

Some libraries have their catalogues on a computer database so you can search by subject. I like to browse through the shelves in the subject area I'm researching. Sometimes I've found very useful books that were not listed in the catalogue.

In addition, many libraries today have CD-ROM searchable disks and other services. Some information may also be on microfiche. Ask your librarian.

Libraries have many valuable resources, including vertical files, directories of people and organizations, statistical abstracts, and encyclopedias. It's a good idea for every writer to browse through the library to gain a basic feel of what is available.

Remember that the sources for your research may vary depending on your readers. For example, if you are writing for a Canadian publication, you'll need to consult the *Canadian Periodical Index*, *Microlog Index*, *Who's Who in Canada*, and the *Directory of Canadian Associations*. Once you take on an assignment in a subject area that you are unfamiliar with, you need a reference librarian to point you toward the proper sources.

Don't forget about specialized libraries, such as law, medical, and business libraries in your city or county. These institutions frequently yield useful material. However, if you are not a member of a particular profession, don't assume you can just walk in and start researching. Instead, call the reference librarian and explain what you want. Ask if it is possible for an outsider to use the library and when. Be sure to say that you are a writer doing research.

This doesn't always work. Once I wanted to look through old files that were no longer in use (i.e., "the morgue") at a newspaper office and I was given an unequivocal "no." I didn't give up. Instead, I wrote a nice letter to the publisher, and he gave me permission.

2.3 Check bibliographies and appendixes

Once you find magazine articles and books on your topic, be sure to take a hard look at their bibliographies and appendixes. You may find a reference or source in the appendix that turns out to be more valuable than the book was.

2.4 Use interlibrary loans

Don't forget the interlibrary loan service. In many areas, your reference librarian can request documents or books for you from other libraries. The cost may be free or minimal.

2.5 Contact clubs, organizations, and trade associations

There are many professional and trade organizations that offer printed information and also help writers identify experts in the field. Check the *Gale Directory* at your library for a vast listing of organizations.

2.6 Network

Tell your friends, colleagues, and relatives what you're working on. I've obtained great leads from newspaper articles that my mother sent me and ones sent by friends and colleagues. Get the word out.

Don't forget to ask your interviewees if they can recommend anyone you should talk to. Ask for telephone numbers. (For more on interviewing, see chapter 11.)

> Networking is the ability to ask for what you want without fear or guilt. The worst that can happen is the person will tell you he or she can't help you, and the best is that he or she may provide excellent contacts.

Discreetly name-drop during the course of a conversation. This doesn't mean bragging about who you know to impress the person. (Although sometimes it doesn't hurt to try to impress, just a little.) Instead, you can often gain more information by mentioning that Dr. X told you such and such and does your interviewee agree with that or not? This is another valuable tactic for gaining good information.

2.7 Use online databases

If you have access to computerized databases, you can find an enormous wealth of information. For example, one database I use is called Northern Lights (www.northernlight.com). On it, I can find a myriad of professional and popular journals as well as unique Web sites. Many Web sites, particularly if they are operated by the government, may have searchable databases. There are also medical databases, such as Medline (www.healthgate.com/medline/search-medline.html), operated by the National Library of Medicine in the United States (See chapter 12 for more on databases.)

Online databases can be valuable, but they often cost money. Government databases are often free but charge for some services. Medline, for example, provides free abstracts, but if I wish to see a complete article, I must pay about US$30 each. There is also a charge for using Northern Lights, although you can obtain a reduced rate if you become a subscriber. Again, abstracts are free but you must pay for entire journal articles. They're fairly inexpensive — from $1 to $2.95 for most articles — which may well be worthwhile if the alternative is heading off to the library on a snowy or rainy night.

If I plan to use an online database, I arrange to have the client reimburse me for that expense. If that is not possible, I factor my estimated search expenses into the amount that I charge the client.

2.8 Online contacts can help too

I have received valuable interview contacts online. For example, for an article on women accountants, I needed to interview someone from the Midwest. I posted an online message to a forum on Compuserve, which netted me a response from a woman who knew a female accountant in Ohio. After screening me through several messages, she gave me the name and number of the accountant. It was a great interview and really made my article.

On another occasion, I read a computer message from a woman who said she was blind and worked for IBM — as a technical writer! Using special equipment, she actually writes software manuals. You can bet my heart beat fast when I read that message. I knew this was a story that I could sell to a magazine for disabled people — and I did.

2.9 Keep learning

Understand that research is never ending; there are always more questions to find answers to. In fact, the more you know about something, the more you realize how little you know.

As you learn about your subject, you may find that what you learn does not support your original presumptions or hypotheses. If the overwhelming burden of evidence shows you were dead wrong about something, do not ignore it. First of all, ignoring your mistake is wrong. Second, readers will pillory you in print for ignoring obvious data.

2.10 Limit your research — if necessary

Remember that your project has a due date and will end, whether it is a year from now or a week from now. Many writers get bogged down because they cannot stop researching and start writing. They keep looking for just one more fact, just one more interview. They know that there is more information out there, and they are right. But the sad truth is that you can never get it all. At a certain point, you have to start writing.

Get as much information as you can within the time and budget allowed. The tighter your budget the more careful you should be about who you call or how far you travel to do your research. Remember, if the project doesn't allow for extra expenses, keep a very close eye on what you spend. Set a limit and don't go over it.

2.11 Get two sources for one fact

Whenever possible, obtain at least two sources for the same fact. Get some backup documentation, either from a magazine or newsletter article, a report, or another expert. This additional work will enhance what you write.

Be sure to jot down citations of facts that you wish to use. It can be very annoying to read "Experts say..." or "The polls say that..." followed by some startling fact. Be more specific.

Also, try to avoid using opinion polls unless you are illustrating beliefs or opinions. What most people think or believe may be dead wrong.

The Internet is a good place to go for documentation to back up facts, but make sure you are getting information from a reputable site.

Ten years ago, few people had heard of the Internet. Today practically everyone is familiar with the term, and writers need to have more than an inkling of how to use this vast repository of information. That's why chapter 12 is about the Internet. But despite all the wonders of the Web, most writers must rely on at least some interviewing of actual people to obtain the information they need. The next chapter provides helpful hints on effective interviewing.

CHAPTER 11

Effective Interviewing

Research usually involves interviewing people, and every writer needs to become a skilled interviewer. If you don't feel you are adept now, don't worry; this is an attainable skill. Just plan ahead, be adaptable, and listen, listen, listen. This chapter covers the basics of interviewing for information.

1. Making contact

Often when you call an interviewee or prospective interviewee, you discover you must reach the person through an assistant, who might ask you what organization you are "with." Many new freelance writers panic at this point, thinking, "I don't really work for the XYZ Corporation, so I can't say I'm *with* them. But on the other hand, I am doing a job for them. But then...." While this internal dialogue is going on, the assistant waits, increasingly suspicious and impatient.

My policy is that if I'm doing a job for a client, I say, "I'm researching an article for the XYZ Corporation." (Because I am!) Then if the secretary or the interviewee asks how come I'm in Florida and the XYZ Corporation is in Boston, I say that this job has been contracted out to me. Businesspeople understand the concept of contracting out because they do it all the time.

I'm not ashamed to say that I'm a freelance writer, but sometimes people's perception of freelance writers as people who are somehow "beyond the fringe" can get in the way. As a result, sometimes I answer the "who are you with" question by stating the name of the organization or agency that I am writing for. Then, when I reach the individual I want to interview, I explain to him or her that I am writing an article on assignment for the organization or agency.

Keep these points in mind when you are calling to arrange an interview:

- Speak confidently, as if you deserve to speak to the other person. Speaking this way makes you *feel* confident, even if you don't start out with that feeling.

- Note the assistant's name. If someone answers, "Ms. Brown's office, Patty Smith speaking," use her name in your response: "Hello Ms. Smith, I'm a writer researching an article for XYZ, and I need to speak with Ms. Brown."

- If Ms. Brown is too busy and you need to call back later, ask for Patty Smith when you call again, and remind her that you need to speak to Ms. Brown. The secret behind this gambit is that a person's name is important. Most assistants and secretaries feel very anonymous within a company.

- Often when you call an organization or business, you will be referred to the "public relations" or "media relations" office. Don't worry, this usually doesn't mean that your interview will never happen. In many cases, media relations people can be very helpful in setting up interviews. Tell them who you are and what you need, and they will usually do their best.

- Set up the interview date and time in advance. Whether it is an in-person interview or a telephone interview, make an appointment — at the interviewee's convenience.

- Be prepared for the possibility that when you call someone to set up an appointment, he or she may say, "Let's do it now!" If the person is otherwise difficult to reach, interviewing him or

My only problem with saying I'm "with" a company is that when I am working on several different jobs, I have to stop for a moment before I make the call and remember who I'm "with" right now!

her on the spot may be necessary. However, in most cases interviewees want to set up a time for the interview because it gives them time to think about what they want to say.

- Set a predetermined place and make sure your interviewee knows the location. If it is in a building, will you meet in the lobby? If it is in a restaurant, will you meet outside? Make sure this is perfectly clear.

- If you will meet in person, give the interviewee a brief description of what you look like. You don't have to supply your height and weight, but try to give some details that will indicate who he should be looking for. "I have red glasses and will be wearing a black dress," or "I have very short hair and will be wearing a blue jacket."

- Give the interviewee your telephone number in case he or she is running late or needs to reschedule.

- For a telephone interview, make sure the interviewee knows it will be by telephone. It often does not occur to people that interviews can and frequently are conducted by telephone. Consequently, some people will be expecting you to appear in person unless you make it very clear this is a telephone interview.

Don't "do lunch" or meet at a bar. First of all, tape recorders pick up all the background noise including other people's conversations, obliterating the one you are trying to conduct. Second, you will both be preoccupied with eating, not spilling, showing you have good manners, and so on. This wastes time.

- Don't hold the interview at your home. If it has to be at someone's home, make it the interviewee's residence. But it's better to meet on neutral turf.

- Tell the interviewee ahead of time how long you think the interview will take, so he or she can schedule enough time. If you need an hour, you don't want to be cut off after 15 minutes.

- Give the interviewee a basic idea of your topic and your slant, but avoid giving all the questions ahead of time. If you give away too much, you're far more likely to get boring "canned" answers that have been preapproved by the public relations department. Sometimes providing the questions up front is the only way to get an interview. If an interviewee imposes this constraint, you need to evaluate if the interview is worth it. If you decide to provide questions ahead of time, during the interview ask the questions you've already submitted — and then slip in a few others that "happen to occur" to you as you talk. In most cases, the interviewee will answer those too, unless your questions are particularly obnoxious or invasive.

2. Pre-interview preparation

Before the interview, read over any material you have on the subject. Your interviewee will not (or should not) expect you to be an expert, but you should try to have a basic grasp of the topic.

Write down the questions you need to cover and that you don't want to forget. Don't think you won't forget them! It is so easy to do so. If one word will jog your memory, use it. Otherwise, write short questions in sentence form. Remember, if the interviewee brings up something that is unique or interesting, it is okay to sacrifice one of your less important questions to get this new information. The preplanned questions are only a guide and not a mandatory script — unless the editor or client has insisted you ask particular questions.

2.1 Create interview questions that work

- Do not phrase the question in a negative way. "You don't think the economy is going to change, do you?" implies that he or she is not supposed to think it's going to change.

- Don't ask the question in a positive way either (i.e., "You do think the economy is going to get better, right?") Don't give away the "right" answer in your question. Presumably, your interviewee is the expert and you are not.

- Try for a neutral approach. "What do you think will happen with the economy over the next six months?" is one possibility. "Where do you see the economy headed?" is acceptable, but your interviewee may then ask what time frame you're talking about. Then you could amend your question and ask about where he or she thinks the economy is headed over the next six months.

📖 Be sure to avoid too many questions that can earn you a meager yes or no. You can't use those responses for quotations. If you do receive a yes or no response, however, press on and ask why, when, and how much.

Samples 5, 6, and 7 show the kind of questions you'd ask a businessperson, the subject of a profile, and someone you're interviewing for a how-to article.

2.2 Be sure your equipment is ready

Does your tape recorder or camera need batteries? Check. Also, if you are conducting an in-person interview, bring an extra tape in case one tape breaks or the person talks for a longer time than you expected. Before the interview, test the recorder to make sure it works. (For more on tape recorders see chapter 13.)

For a telephone interview, slide in a tape and check that it records the telephone busy signal, or call up the time and temperature number or the weather report and see if it records well.

Take the telephone off the hook before the designated time so that you don't get caught by an incoming call.

3. Conducting the interview

Many people are afraid to be interviewed. They may have been misquoted in the past or they may be generally fearful of the media. It is part of your job to put this person sufficiently at ease so he or she will answer your questions. This does not mean your interview subject has to become your new best friend, but try to maintain an open and genial attitude. (Investigative reporting is the one exception to this rule.)

If the interview is in person, you will probably have to spend a few moments accepting or declining coffee, chatting about the weather, and so on. If the interview is by telephone, social niceties can usually be rapidly dispensed with and you can get down to business fast. This is one reason why I prefer telephone interviews.

I am bolding the next statement so you won't miss it. **Ask the easy questions first.** These are the ones your interviewee should not mind

Interview Questions to Ask a Businessperson

1. What is the hardest part about this job (or industry, field, etc.)? Why do you consider it the hardest part?

2. What is the biggest mistake people in this field make?

3. Where do you see this field (or your career) headed over the next three to five years? Why?

4. What do you like best about this field? Why?

5. What is a typical day like for you?

6. What are the trends in this field? Why?

7. There is no way you could tell me everything you know about this subject. But is there anything we haven't discussed that you think is important for readers to know? (Define who your readers are: human resources executives, teachers, etc.)

8. Who else in this field do you recommend that I contact?

9. What is the most surprising aspect of _____ (your topic)?

Interview Questions For a Profile Subject

1. Where were you born and raised?

2. When you were growing up, did you ever imagine that some day you'd become a _____ (e.g., successful executive, famous ballerina)?

3. What is a typical day like for you?

4. What personality trait makes you successful?

5. What is the hardest part of your job?

6. What would you change about your career field if you had magical powers?

7. What is the most fulfilling aspect of your career?

8. Where do you hope to be five years from now?

9. What are your hobbies?

10. Who is your favorite author?

11. Who do you admire most?

12. Did you have a mentor in your career? Who was it and what did he or she do?

Questions For a How-To Interview

1. How long did it take you to learn how to _____ (e.g., build log cabins, grow rare orchids)?

2. How long would it take the average person?

3. What is the best part about learning how to do this?

4. What is the hardest part?

5. What materials do you need?

6. Describe the process for me, from start to finish.

7. Does a person need any special training or equipment to achieve this goal?

8. What is the biggest mistake people doing this make? Are there any others?

---

answering. Ask hard questions in the middle, and leave the ones you can live without at the end. Why? Because you need those hard questions answered, and if you leave them to the end, you may never get to them because of time constraints and other issues.

Why not ask the hard questions first? Because they may scare the person off. It's better to ease your way toward them than to jump right in.

3.1 Take notes

Even though I recommend taping interviews, I also recommend taking notes during an interview because as the person talks, you may think of a question. Write it down and ask it later.

Another reason to take notes is that the tape recorder cannot give you a physical description of the person, so you must jot these details down if they are important. Smoothing away imaginary dust, staring off into space, and other gestures an interviewee may make are details that can reveal character to a reader.

Always check the spelling of a person's name. It doesn't matter what the name is. Sometimes "John Smith" is really "Jon Smyth." Even the most ordinary-sounding names may have a special spelling. Also make sure you get his or her full and proper title at work, if that is important.

3.2 The bones of an interview

Let's walk through a hypothetical interview to look at its bare bones.

Your first interview is at the XYZ Corporation at 9:00 a.m. You arrive five minutes early. This is good. (If you are *too* early, for example 20 or 30 minutes or more, ride around the block or sit in your car. If you are — horrors — late, apologize profusely and don't blame anyone else.)

You tell the receptionist you have an appointment to speak with Ms. Wonderful. You decline the offer of coffee or accept it, depending on what you prefer.

Ms. Wonderful comes out, greets you, and leads you back to her office. She offers you a chair and looks at you expectantly. You tell her (again, although you told her before) that you are writing a piece for the *Marvelous* magazine and your basic angle is the female executive in male-dominated fields. She recalls having talked with you.

Now you set up your tape recorder, preferably between you and her so that both your voices will come through clearly. If she is seated behind her desk and the distance between you is too great, get closer. Move your chair or ask her to move.

Don't ask permission to use the tape recorder. Unless she is blind, she can see what it is. Conversely, when it's a telephone interview, the interviewee cannot see the recorder. You don't ask permission then either, but do announce that you are taping the interview. State that you are doing this for accuracy and start your questions. Most interviewees have no problem with being taped. (If they do, stress that you are recording the conversation to make sure you don't make a mistake or misquote the person.)

If there are any pauses in conversation or your interviewee is called away for a few moments, rewind the tape a little bit and make sure it is recording. (I have been known to bring two recorders to an interview, but that is usually not necessary.)

At the end of the interview, ask if there is anything else your interviewee wants to add. I will close with a question like: "Ms. X, you've given me so much valuable information. There's no way you can tell me everything there is to know on this subject, since you are the expert, but is there anything we haven't discussed that you think is important for readers to know?"

This is also when you could network, asking your subject to refer you to other experts: "Mr. Y, you have a vast amount of knowledge on this topic, but I need to interview a few other people as well. I can't imagine anyone knowing as much as you do, but is there anyone you would recommend who I should contact?" Your interviewee will usually be flattered by your comments and give you at least one or two names — ask for telephone numbers, too. (Then, when you call Ms. Z, be sure to say that Mr. Y recommended you call. Often the mention of the other expert's name is enough to whet the interest of the new subject.)

Be sure to thank the person. I do this effusively, and usually make a positive comment about how lucky the industry or field is to have such a dedicated person involved.

3.3 Categorizing interviews

From my experience (and I'm not sure why this is true), interviews are either easy or difficult. They are not so-so. For a novice, all interviews may be difficult. They should never all be easy or you're doing something wrong — there needs to be an edge to at least some of your interviews. It helps to keep you on your toes.

3.3.a Easy interviews

Many interviews are a pleasure. This is particularly true if you are profiling someone who wants to be written about or interviewing an expert who loves his or her field.

Sometimes you need only listen and guide the interviewee every once in awhile if he or she strays off the topic. Other times you will

> As much as possible, maintain a neutral stance and don't let your own opinions or views intrude. The purpose of an interview is to get information and good quotes; it's not just a conversation.

need to ask many questions, but these may be ones that are obvious and it will be easy to get answers.

However, you can never assume an interview that starts off easily will continue that way, and you can never turn off your listening ears.

Let your interviewee dominate the interview, but don't be afraid to interrupt if he or she is stuck in talk-only mode. You need information and you have a limited time in which to gather it. If your interviewee keeps rushing off on a tangent, don't stay silent. Most people stop to take a breath once in awhile; when that happens, ask your next question.

3.3.b Difficult interviews

An interview can be difficult because you feel uncomfortable with the subject or have some other problem. This is something you can work on. Familiarize yourself with the topic and then quit worrying.

More frequently, interviews can be difficult because the interviewed person is uncomfortable or upset. No matter how effective an interviewer you are and how wonderful you are as a person, there will inevitably be times when people do not want to talk with you. The problem is that you need to do the interview.

If you find yourself in this situation, one tactic is to try to find out why the person doesn't want to talk with you. It may be a bad time for the interviewee, or he or she might not feel well or be facing a personal crisis. You may never find out the reason.

Some people are afraid to talk to journalists because they fear being misquoted and risking their position. Maybe this person has been misquoted in the past and has suffered considerably.

When I encounter this fear (and you can usually tell when people are afraid of being interviewed by their behavior, tone of voice, and lack of eye contact), I tell the person that I am not Mike Wallace of *60 Minutes* and I am not seeking out their deepest darkest fears. (This is true, by the way — I don't do dramatic investigative reporting that exposes malfeasance.)

If you have set up an interview but are receiving clear signs that the person is not receptive to it, for whatever reason, it may be a good idea to reschedule it.

Often, this statement is a great disarmer, and the person usually responds with laughter, in part because I am a woman, so of course I am not Mike Wallace. And also in part because it gets the fear out in the open, which eases it.

I tell my interview subjects that I tape record all interviews because I want to make sure I get the quotes *right*. In addition, I tell them that the only time I change quotes is when a person makes a misstatement and says "are" instead of "is" or makes some other small grammatical error.

3.4 Effective listening

Good writers are — or should learn to be — good listeners. It's a very important skill that will enable you to elicit far more information than those other writers who are not good listeners.

Many people think they are effective at listening, but studies have revealed that much of what is said never reaches our brains. We start out intending to be good listeners; we watch the person's body language, listen to the tone of voice, and try to follow the words. Then our concentration slips and we start thinking about our own internal dialogue. Resist this tendency! Don't try to shut off the internal dialogue but instead, focus it on what the person is saying. Try the following tactics:

(a) Sometimes you may hear noises outside or the room may be too hot or too cold. If you can control these things, do so. Ask if you can shut the window. Put on your jacket if you're cold or take it off if you're hot. If you don't have control, ignore these things.

(b) Your interviewee's appearance or behavior may distract you. For this reason, try ahead of time to identify your own personal distracters, whether it is a person's dress, accent, or words and phrases that annoy you. For example, I loathe the phrase, "He's dead meat!" If you know what your personal distracters are, you can think to yourself, "Oh there I go again, thinking about that phrase that annoys me. I must concentrate on what he is saying."

(c) Go for content. Consider the behavioral tics, outlandish clothing, or annoying slang to be a sort of packaging. What you really

Two people could interview the same person at the same time and hear exactly the same words. The better listener gains much more.

need is inside the package — the main point or points of what the person is saying. Keep in mind that something wonderful can be sloppily wrapped and draped over with a hideous orange bow. But inside the package there could be a beautiful diamond necklace or gold watch. You are looking for informational gems in your interviewee and nearly everyone has at least one. Seek that out and don't worry about the packaging.

Here are a few other basic tips for effective listening:

- Paraphrase what you think the subject has said to you. "Mr. Jones, it sounds as if within the next two years, your company may well be number one in your field." If you're wrong, he'll tell you. If you're off-course, he'll tell you. And if you're dead-on, he'll tell you.

- Do not be afraid to be wrong or confused about something. It is better to ask a question that you may consider "stupid" than to write something wrong and annoy your editor, interviewee, and readers later on.

- Are there trends and changes in the interviewee's field? Do not worry about memorizing quantities and statistics. You should be taping these figures anyway. Instead, try to determine what the statistics or figures mean: are things better or worse? Always ask for an explanation. Again, don't be afraid of seeming stupid because you don't understand something.

- Get the interviewee to explain any jargon or special terms; your readers will want to know what they mean.

- If an interviewee evades your question, ask it again later, re-worded.

- Listen and watch for emotion. If the person is stating that everything is wonderful, but he is frowning or looks angry, you'll need to do some additional probing. You could say something like, "Mr. Ex, you just told me that sales are up 47% but then you frowned. I'm wondering if you were really hoping for even greater sales or if there was some other issue — such as expenses had to increase a lot to get to that point."

- Give the person time to answer. Too many interviewers ask a question and then keep talking. Ask your question. And then shut up. Most people cannot stand silence; as an interviewer, you can use this fact to help you. Your only response, during breaks, should be affirmative comments such as "Yes, I see."

- If the person talks too long, stop making affirming comments. If necessary, cough or gaze distractedly away. Most people catch on. Try to avoid interrupting unless you must. When your interviewee pauses, try to summarize what has been said: "It sounds like you are saying that..." and listen to see if you got it right.

3.4.a Listening skills for the in-person interview

- Eye contact is important, but don't stare!

- Notice where the interviewee sits. Does the interviewee hide behind a big desk, sit next to you, or stand and look down upon you? These are all clues to the person.

At some point in the interview, say something positive. Unless you're interviewing a mass murderer, you should be able to find something positive to say that you believe is true. Never make insincere small talk. Sadly, most people are starved for positive feedback. The slightest favorable comment can often elicit a great deal of information.

3.4.b Listening skills for the telephone interview

- Make an appointment for the telephone interview, just as you would for an in-person interview. Tell the person you have recorded this date on your calendar and ask him or her to record it as well. Give your telephone number.

- When you call up for the interview, be polite and friendly but keep any small talk to a minimum.

- Listen for changes in voice; be sensitive to changes in pitch. If the person starts to fade out, you can try speaking very softly, which tends to make people speak up, or you can start talking more loudly. You can also try asking the interviewee to speak up.

- If the person rambles on and on, be completely silent. Most people will stop talking. Silence also works after you ask a question. Ask it and shut up and listen.

- Don't be afraid if your interviewee is silent for a few moments; he or she may be framing an answer. Give the interviewee a chance to answer.

- Sometimes you must interrupt because you need to get your interviewee back on track. Always be polite; an interview is an exchange between two professionals, not a social occasion.

4. Reflections on interviewing and interviewees

Based on my nearly 20 years' experience of interviewing people, it seems to me that a person's occupation can indicate whether he or she will be easy or difficult to interview. Your experience may prove different, but let me share what I have learned to date.

In my experience, police officers have proven to be the most difficult people to interview. They are the most challenging subjects to extract information from. This may be because police officers often deal with people who lie to them. I have spent inordinate amounts of time working to convince a police officer that I would not misquote him or her and that I would use the information to a good end.

So how do you interview a cop? Make arrangements well ahead of time, tell him or her exactly what you want to do and why, and show up on time for the interview.

Conversely, I have found lawyers to be very easy to interview. It could be because lawyers think they could sue me if they don't like what I write, but I don't really think that's it. Lawyers are very verbal people and are used to communicating information. They are also very analytical.

As you might guess, politicians are generally easy to interview, as long as you don't need to nail them down on specifics. If you ask them to discuss their views in general, they are wonderful interviewees. Most politicians want press and it's easy to obtain access to them. (Of course, it's far more difficult to arrange an interview with a president or prime minister.) Call the politician's press secretary and explain why you want to interview the politician and who you are writing the piece for. If it is a magazine, you will probably be asked what its circulation is, so find out ahead of time.

Physicians are fairly easy to interview, but it is hard to find a time when you can actually talk to one. Telephone interviews are best when you want to interview a doctor.

College and university professors are not difficult to interview, but they often love to expound on theory. You must keep them on track to get practical details. If you do an in-person interview, you may find the professor lecturing at you as if you were a student. Let him or her go on if you are getting useful data. If not, interrupt with your questions.

Sometimes highly educated people who are affluent are more worried about their status and how what they say might possibly affect them. They may worry about getting fired or not getting promoted if they're rising stars in the corporation. Expect that they will refer you to the public relations department and sometimes try to duck an interview altogether. Try to disarm such a person with honesty and charm; some you'll never win over, and you must accept this.

Tradespeople and nonprofessionals are often initially a little nervous about being interviewed, but they are far less timorous than those who have, or think they have, a lot to lose.

I cannot generalize by gender. Some men are tough to interview and some are easy, and women are the same. Women often speak too softly and your tape recorder may not pick up everything. You can either ask soft-spoken people to speak up or speak very softly yourself, so that they ask you to speak up. This makes them speak up.

I think people over age 40 are generally easier to interview, but that may be in part because I am over age 40. Retired people are frequently eager to be interviewed, possibly because they have more time and also because they want to share their experiences with others.

In my experience, children under the age of 12 are too squirmy and easily distracted to be good interviewees. Adolescents are too worried about their appearance and how their peers will react to what they say, so I generally try avoiding interviews with teenagers as well.

Sometimes people from other countries can be difficult to interview because they don't know the right words to convey their thoughts or they're afraid that they don't know them. They may underestimate their own abilities. Avoid using "slanguage" when speaking with someone from another country. If he or she uses a term you are not familiar with, ask politely for an explanation.

If the interview is not going in the direction you want and you are unable to interrupt and get it back on track, use silence to work for you (as mentioned earlier). Don't use words that encourage continuation, such as "Really?" "Oh?" Say nothing. Most people become uncomfortable and stop talking.

5. Solutions to common interview problems

5.1 Overprotective assistant

The assistant protects the boss from all evil invaders, especially those who telephone.

Solution: Be self-confident but not arrogant. Explain what you're trying to do: for example, "I'm researching an article on X for *Miracle Magazine*." Explain how much time you need. In most cases, you won't need more than an hour. Politely ask when would be a good time to call. If the assistant says "never" (most would not say this, but there are some diehards), then laugh to signify you know she is joking and offer alternative times. Late afternoon? Right after work starts? Lunchtime? Get the assistant's name.

The next time you call, ask for the assistant or secretary by name. State that you are the person who called yesterday and wondered if Mr. Wonderful might be available this week to talk with you. Always be polite and friendly. It usually works!

5.2 Interviewee wants a veto

The interviewee asks to see the article or the manuscript before submission or wants to approve any quotes. However, your editor says that you never, ever show your copy to anybody else. Think about who is paying you: the editor.

Solution: Tell your interviewee that you will tape the interview (and I think you should) and that you are very careful when it comes to accuracy. You can explain that many writers, including reporters from major newspapers, do not tape and this is probably one reason why people may sometimes get misquoted.

I also assure my interviewees that the only changes I make to quotes are minor rewordings to correct grammar. This is very appreciated and relieves most people.

5.3 Evasive interviewee

You've asked a question and the interviewee has not answered. Instead he or she has responded by talking about something else. This is very common among politicians and people who are media savvy.

Solution: Ask several other questions, then reframe your original and unanswered question, using different words. Try up to three times. If this doesn't work, you're probably not going to get the answer. You could come right out and ask about it, saying, "It seems that one question I've asked you is a problem. I know our readers will wonder about this question, and the editor is bound to ask me about it, too. I can't figure out what to say." Sometimes this works.

5.4 Getting confidential information

You need some information and the interviewee has said that he or she is not going to give it to you. For example, you need to know about how much the company grossed last year, and the interviewee says that is confidential information.

Solution: You probably have at least a vague feel of how much the company makes. Let's say you think it's around $20 million. Say to the reluctant interviewee, "I understand, but we need a rough ballpark figure for our readers. So I'm guessing you're at around $10 million."

In most cases, the interviewee will forget all about confidentiality and say, "What?! $10 million! We grossed $21.47 million last year and this year we're going to top $23 million!" At this point you are very impressed and apologize for accidentally slighting the company. Now that you have it right, you assure him or her, you won't make that mistake.

CHAPTER 12

Using the Internet

Whether or not you like the Internet, and whether or not you are adept at using it, the fact is that many writers and editors rely on the Internet to obtain a large part of their information. In addition, many of us, including me, use the Internet to find clients and to communicate with our clients by electronic mail. Sometimes I send entire articles or chapters via e-mail because a client is in a rush and a courier is just not fast enough. (A fax is fast but does not provide the receiver with an electronic version of the file that he or she can edit.)

The Internet is not new — it has been around for many years — but it has only been in the past decade or so that Internet usage has surged forward. Prior to that, only individuals who were technically savvy found the Internet useful — or usable. Now, with every passing day, the Internet becomes an indispensable tool for more and more business-people and for writers.

There are a broad array of Web sites for writers, including sites offered by individuals, organizations, magazines, and newsletters. Some are excellent, some are okay, and some are a waste of time. There are also sites that concentrate heavily on jobs for writers. I have listed some sites in the Appendix for you to consider.

Yet many people are terrified of plunging into the world of the Internet, acting as if they are city people entering a primeval forest, fearful of unknown and unseen threats in all directions. I have trained clients who were neurologists, pediatricians, and other very intelligent people on how to receive and send electronic mail and how to perform other basic Internet tasks. Despite their initial trepidation, as well as an overly active fear of seeming stupid, these individuals quickly mastered the basics. The point is, it's normal to be scared, but it's really not as awful as you imagine. Read on for more information.

1. Learning the basics

Here are the basics that a writer needs to know about the Internet. If you want to learn more, there are many books dedicated to the subject.

- Many businesses and government organizations have Web sites.

- Many organizations provide searchable databases of all their written material.

- Some Web sites appear amateurish but may have useful information.

- Some sites look beautiful and slick, but the information is useless, old, or bad.

- You'll never fully master the Internet. There's just too much going on. You can, however, gain a great deal of good information

- The opinion or agendas of individual Web sites may not always be apparent.

1.1 Businesses and government organizations

Whether at the state, provincial, or some other level of government, every day more governmental agencies and organizations get on the Internet with their special sections, called "Web sites."

Many businesses are on the Net too. Small businesses seemed to gravitate to the Internet first, while large established businesses bemusedly watched. Now many of those same large companies have decided that they must have a presence on the Web.

A few words about Web sites

Usually the first page you see on a Web site is the "home page," which is the root or main page of a Web site. There are countless pages on the World Wide Web. Some have valuable information while others rehash material that was written 10 or 20 years ago. Just because it's on the Internet does not mean that it was written five minutes ago.

If you want to visit a specific Web site, you need its address or URL (which stands for Uniform Resource Locator). The URL identifies a Web site, much as a name, street address, and so forth are used to identify where a business or home is located. If you read about a business or product with the address "www.cashews.com" (I made this up, but it may well exist), and you want to find out more about it, you must tell your web browser where to go by typing out "http://www.cashews.com." Most people don't include the "http://" in the address because it is considered a given. However, if you are new to the Internet, how could you know this? (Now you do.)

There are some addresses that do not have a "www" in them. Instead, an address may be, for example, "pecans.com/". If there is no www in the address, do not add it or you won't get to the Web site.

The Blair Witch Project, a low-budget film that some say has grossed over $140 million, was promoted heavily on the Internet. Now mainstream moviemakers have decided they need to have a presence on the Worldwide Web.

1.2 Organizations with searchable databases

Some government agencies and businesses offer searchable databases replete with a wealth of information. What's a searchable database? It's a computerized repository of articles, a bit like an online library. Using "keywords," you are led to the articles that include your keyword and are (hopefully) what you are looking for.

You can use simple keyword searches with one word, such as "adoption," although I wouldn't advise using that word if you were interested in the adoption of children, since an article could refer to the adoption of a law. (Or of a pet. Or even of a highway!) In such cases you may prefer to use two words or combination of words, such as "adopted children" or (adopted children) AND (international). There are numerous combinations you can try.

Once you choose your keywords and click on the "search" button of the database, your search will start and usually end in seconds. The database will then tell you how many "hits" you've received, which means how many times your keyword(s) appeared in articles in the database. If you have more than 10,000 hits, you probably should use different words.

It's impossible to list all the available databases, but you can search government organizations and private company databases on a broad array of topics in the United States and Canada as well as many other countries.

1.3 Appearances can be deceptive

Some Web sites are very impressive, yet their content leaves much to be desired. The client may have hired a Web designer to make a beautiful Web site and provided little in terms of actual content.

Conversely, some Web sites may look like a child prepared them, yet the information is timely and accurate. You will need more than a cursory look to make a judgment on any given Web site.

1.4 You'll never understand it all

You will be permanently frustrated if you think you can master the entire Internet quickly and easily. Or ever. You can learn a great deal and become extremely adept. But more information is constantly being added. For this reason, I listen to my fellow writers when they recommend a new "search engine" (see section **3.** below).

1.5 Opinions and agendas are not always clear

Some Web sites on the Internet are run by individuals or groups with very specific views. Often it is easy to see their underlying bias. Other times, groups present information that is slanted toward their view, but they are much more cagey about what that view is. They may pretend that they are stating facts rather than opinions.

This tactic is fairly obvious when flamboyant statements with lots of exclamation marks and bold type are used. It is less obvious when the site is understated and resembles research.

If you have any doubts about information on the Web, double-check it. In fact, double-check even if you don't have doubts. It's good to have at least two, preferably more, independent verifications of the same material.

Many Web sites have "links" to other sites. Don't use one of these linked sites as your verification point. The sites that are linked are probably sites that support the viewpoint of the group you are checking up on. Look elsewhere.

Warning for Newbies

Warning: There's plenty of pornography on the Internet, and you don't have to go looking for it — the porn purveyors will find you when you use the Net, even if you merely looked up completely innocent material. (It's too complicated to explain how they track you.) They then send E-mails asking you if you're interested in lewd pictures of "teenage girls" and so forth.

What should you do when this happens? Delete the e-mail. That's about all you can do, although some Internet Service Providers instruct you to forward all "spam" (unwanted junk e-mail) to them.

2. Tools you will need

Many local newspapers offer weekly columns on computer topics, and the *Wall Street Journal* frequently discusses new hardware and software options.

To get online, you'll need a computer and a modem (see chapter 13). You'll also need an Internet service provider (ISP). An ISP is a link between your computer and the Internet. There are far too many ISPs to name them all. You could sign up with America Online or CompuServe, or you could use a local service in your hometown. Some large companies have entered the ISP area. For example, some telephone companies have an Internet service provider division.

Whether the company you are considering is a large multinational conglomerate or a service offered in your city, ask for a brochure or pamphlet and read it. Find out what the terms and conditions of service are. Generally you pay some monthly fee for this service, so check out what this monthly rate is, how much time online this allows you, and what other services will be provided.

Find out how technically based the service is. If you are not a "techie," go for the simplest service available.

Check how long you have to sign up for. Don't commit to a year if you can avoid it, because you might try the service and hate it. Ask if you can have a trial of 30 days instead. At the end of 30 days, if you are happy, you can make a longer-term commitment.

Most services allow you to charge your payment on your credit card, but if necessary, you may be able to arrange for payment by check or money order.

Be sure that your ISP offers an electronic mail option. Otherwise, you'll have to buy e-mail service as an add-on or sign on to another ISP for your e-mail. When possible, it's best to go with one service.

3. Searching the Internet

3.1 Searching for free with search engines

There are many different "search engines" that you can use to find information. Most allow you to type in a keyword that the search engine will then use to find information for you, whether the topic is business- or government-related or something else altogether.

The search engine leads you to sites on the World Wide Web that have information related to your keywords. It rushes quickly through thousands of pages of data until it finds a "hit" — a place or places where your keyword is found. The more common the keyword, the more hits you will find, and often you will need to redo your search to narrow down your options.

It's a good idea to use more than one search engine. If the material you want can't be found using one search engine, it may be available through another one. Here are a few search engines that I have found useful.

(a) *Ask Jeeves (www.askjeeves.com)*. When you use this search engine, the picture of a butler appears. You ask the butler a question and it will do its search, usually coming back with several possible sites for you to select from. This is a fast search engine and can be very useful.

(b) *Inference.com (www.infind.com)*. Another useful tool is Inference.com, which searches many sources for you within 30 seconds or less. (You set the timer.) It may come up with some of the same sites as Ask Jeeves but it may also include others that Jeeves never thought of.

(c) *Fedworld (www.fedworld.gov)*. If you want to know about what's going on in the US government, Fedworld is a good choice to help you seek out many different possible federal agencies. You can search Web pages and government reports.

(d) *Medline (www.healthgate.com/medline/search-medline.shtml)*. Medline is a medical database offered by the US National Library of Medicine on a Web site called "Healthgate." Its span is great — about 9 million articles in English and other languages from many different countries, including Canada and the United States. The database goes back about 30 years and is updated rapidly.

If you are researching a medical topic, you can search Medline for free and obtain free abstracts. But if you want the full text, you must pay for the article. Articles are pricey (about US$30). For this reason, I usually ask my reference librarian at the public library if she can order these articles for me. If she can't, and if I can't find them in the nearest college library, sometimes I need the article so much that I must pay the fee.

You can get an account on Medline using your credit card. Orders are usually encrypted so that the world can't see what your credit card number is, but you can check this for yourself.

(e) *Book databases.* One of my favorite search tools is Amazon.com, which includes virtually every book in print in its database. I like this database because it's easy to search and it offers a "page" on each book, including information on the author, the publisher, date of publication, and a picture of the book. It also includes a description of the book. (See chapter 5 for a description of how I use Amazon.com to research the competition section of a book proposal.) If you want to order any of the books on Amazon.com, it's very easy to do so. I like using the following Web address because it is the page you can use to search by author, title, or subject: www.amazon.com/exec/obidos/ats-query-page/.

Barnes and Noble (www.bn.com/index.asp) also has a good book search service, and it's also free. I like this service because you can do a search by keyword and request that the books it finds are listed either in bestselling order or in order of publication, with the newest ones first. It also offers a page per book. One feature that Barnes and Noble has, which Amazon.com lacks, is its excellent out-of-print search section. You can locate hard-to-find books on that service. The books are offered by a variety of booksellers, but if you decide to purchase, you order through Barnes and Noble and they take care of the transaction. I have ordered several books and all were in very good condition, even though some were ten years old.

These two sites are not the entire breadth of book search sites — there are many more. They just happen to be my personal favorites and I think you will find them highly useful too.

3.2 Searching for nonfree: When you have to pay

If you are willing to spend some money, there are many more possibilities to consider, though I generally try to avoid paying whenever possible!

(a) *Northern Lights (usgovsearch.northernlight.com).* I like Northern Lights because it will give me a list of journal articles, newspapers, Web sites, and other possibilities to consider. I can receive article abstracts for free. If I want full text, I must pay, but the fee is usually $2.95 and sometimes it's as low as $1. This is currently my favorite database. I have found a great deal of information using it. I used Northern Lights to update a book on child abuse for the original authors, to obtain the most recent articles on adoption, and to research medical problems such as gastroesophageal reflux disease (GERD) for a book my physician coauthor and I will have out in 2001. I also used it to research attention deficit disorder, another one of my book topics.

To use this database, you will need to provide your e-mail address and your credit card number. You can choose the secure option (I do!) so that the information will be encrypted when you send it.

(b) *UnCoverWeb (uncweb.carl.org)*. Another search tool that I have found useful is UnCoverWeb. You can search for free and obtain citations and abstracts. If you want full text, it can be pricey — $26 or more per article, depending on the particular piece. I use this service to obtain abstracts and then if I want full text, I ask my reference librarian at the public library to obtain them for me.

3.3 Searching usenet groups

Another way to gather information, albeit more informally, is by sending a message stating your topic to a usenet group. A usenet group is a public e-mail system. There are hundreds of usenet groups on myriad topics, ranging from groups interested in *Babylon 5* (an old television show) to groups for people fascinated by every possible aspect of politics to other individuals enamored of the most trivial topics you can imagine. (Of course, if it's important to *you*, it doesn't seem like a trivial topic.)

Users of usenet groups leave messages about a topic and read the responses later on at their leisure. Some people "lurk" and only read messages and responses. That is perfectly okay.

Ask your ISP how to access usenet groups. Nearly all ISPs enable usenet access, but the way they do it may vary.

How do you find out what usenet groups are of interest to you? You can search all usenet groups with keywords using the Deja.com search engine. If your subject is anywhere on a usenet group, this special search engine will find out. If Deja.com doesn't come up with anything, try varying your keyword. I usually try a few different keywords before I give up.

Once you find a usenet group that interests you, select the "subscribe" option. You can then read all messages, respond to them, or create your own message thread. (A thread is a string of messages with the same subject title and includes the original message and all the responses.) Later, if you wish, you can "unsubscribe."

It's not hard to create a message; merely follow the menu directions that are provided.

3.4 Listservs

List servers, also known as listservs, are different from usenet groups. If you sign up for a listserv, you will receive every message that is written and they will all be sent to you by e-mail. This can become extremely cumbersome! (For some listserv newsletters of interest to writers, see the Appendix.)

If you're going to use a listserv, it's a good idea to get yourself another e-mail address that you will only use for listserv messages. Yahoo.com offers free e-mail accounts, as does Hotmail.com. America Online allows users to use more than one e-mail address. Why should you do this? Because you will know that the messages to that address are from the listserv and they won't clutter up your regular e-mailbox.

When I was researching eldercare for my *Unofficial Guide to Eldercare* (Macmillan, 1999), I requested admission to an Alzheimer's listserv. I must have received at least 30 to 40 messages per day from people contributing to this group, but it was worth reading their messages because I obtained valuable information as well as a "feel" for what it was like to be a caregiver to a person with Alzheimer's Disease. When I completed my research, I "unsubscribed" and my daily volume of e-mail dropped dramatically!

I also used a listserv while researching my book *Moms with Attention Deficit Disorder* (Prima Publishing, in press for 2000). In this case, I subscribed to "addwomen," reading messages and asking questions. In addition, I recruited mothers with ADD to respond to my questionnaire (see Sample 8, which I sent by e-mail to each respondent privately — and they replied to me privately.)

3.5 Obtaining information by creating your own surveys

A technique I developed myself, and one that I use frequently, is to create my own questionnaires and then go online to usenet groups on the Internet or forums on CompuServe and America Online and find people to answer them. I post a message, telling people I am a writer looking for individuals to comment on the subject I am researching. I assure anonymity because most of my publishers only want direct quotations from experts. I find that people are more candid when they don't have to worry about being quoted by name.

If I receive sufficient response (at least 5 to 10 people within a day), then I send out the questionnaire and ask them to e-mail it back to me.

I try to ask questions that will elicit more than a "yes" or "no" response. If I ask an opinion question, I ask why the respondent thinks what he or she has stated. Some people write many pages and others answer the questions very simply.

I have created questionnaires for women with migraine headaches or attention deficit disorder, adoptive parents, people caring for aging parents, and many other groups.

These are not scientific questionnaires. I don't need a control group, nor must I abide by other clinical parameters. I'm a writer seeking information and I make that clear. Sometimes I seek the information on behalf of another person such as a physician, and in that case, I say so, but the individuals send their responses to me.

Once I was researching an article for a trade magazine on careers in mining, so I created a questionnaire for people in the mining industry. But where to place the notice of my questionnaire? Using a search engine, I found the Web site of a mining consulting firm. When I contacted the owner by e-mail (his e-mail was listed on the Web site), he allowed me to leave my questionnaire on his site. I asked people to respond to me by e-mail. All the Web site owner wanted was some simple (for me) research that he wasn't sure how to do. I did the research for him and he was happy. In return, I received e-mail from all over the globe — it was overwhelming in a wonderful kind of way.

When I write the book or article, I quote from the responses to my questionnaires, making up names for the respondents. (I use first names only.) Sometimes I change their gender too, making a John into a Jane. If the person's age is important, I may use the actual age with the pretend name.

Is it a "self-selected" group of people responding to me? Sure it is. It is also usually a group of people with a great interest in and concern about my topic. I can't imagine any other way I could find such a group of people so fast.

What do I usually ask in my questionnaire? It depends on the topic, but generally I ask the following generic questions:

- What is the hardest thing about it?

- What is the most surprising thing about it?

- What are the major myths associated with it?

- What is the most important thing to know about it?

- How has it affected your daily life?

I always ask the respondent if there is anything that I have not asked that is important to know — this question has netted me extremely valuable responses (see the questionnaire in Sample 8).

Sometimes I find a question that I thought was a good one is misunderstood or is confusing and I can see that from my initial responses. So I clarify it or delete it.

Can you use my questionnaire technique? I don't see why not. Be honest, tell respondents your real name and what your real topic is, and let them know that you are writing a book or article or report on this topic. Promise them anonymity if you plan to offer it. (You must not renege on this promise.) Some people want their names in the article; if so, they will tell you. You may not wish to use them unless they are experts or their names are important for some other reason.

Sometimes you will think of questions you wish you had asked. You may decide to ask some respondents if they will answer a few follow-up questions, and most will accommodate you. Once.

There are disadvantages to my online questionnaire/ survey. Sometimes people will send you silly answers and sometimes people will deride you for a variety of reasons. You can ignore them or you can try explaining what you are doing. But ignoring usually works better.

Sample Questionnaire

Questionnaire For Moms With Attention Deficit Disorder (With or Without Hyperactivity)
Created by Christine Adamec as research for her book

Note: Your name will not be used in this book. Only the names of physicians or other professionals in the field will be used.

1. Have you been diagnosed with Attention Deficit Disorder?

    _____Yes

    _____No

2. If the answer to Question 1 is "yes," were you diagnosed by a:

    _____psychiatrist

    _____other medical doctor

    _____psychologist

    _____other expert (please state what type.)_____

3. How old are you now? _____ (Remember, I don't use real names, so the world will never know it's you — because I'm not telling!)

4. How old were you when you were diagnosed?_____

5. Has your child(ren) been diagnosed with ADD also?

    _____Yes

    _____No

6. If you are married, does your husband have Attention Deficit Disorder?

    _____Yes

    _____No

    _____Not married

7. Are you mostly:

_____hyperactive

_____inattentive

_____about equally hyper and inattentive

8. Please select from the following areas in which you have some problems. Choose as many as apply.

_____Concentration

_____Organization

_____Impulsivity

_____Distractibility

_____Forgetfulness

_____Neatness

_____Others (Please write in what they are here.)_____

9. Do you think that society has expectations of mothers that are sometimes hard for moms with ADD to meet?

_____Yes

_____No

_____Not sure

10. If you answered "Yes" to Question 9, what does society expect of mothers that can be hard for moms with ADD?

11. Do you think society is generally more accepting of boys or men with ADD than of girls or women?

_____Yes

_____No

_____Not sure

12. What makes you think your answer to Question 11 is true? Can you think of any examples?

13. Do you think teachers are understanding of moms with ADD?

_____Yes

_____No

_____Don't know

14. Why do you respond as you did to Question 13? What experiences have highlighted the problem to you?

15. Do you think ADD moms have more or less guilt than the average mother has about her parenting abilities?

_____More

_____Less

_____About the same

16. Please elaborate on your answer in Question 15.

17. How old are your children?

18. Do you have a career in addition to the job of being a mother?

_____Yes

_____No

19. If yes to Question 19, what is your career field?_____

20. Is this career field "friendly" or unfriendly to a woman with ADD? Please explain.

_____Friendly

_____So-so

_____Not friendly

21. Do you think/worry about your children a lot on the job and then think about the job a lot when you are with your children?

_____Yes

_____No

22. What is the hardest thing about being a mom with ADD?

23. What is the thing that has surprised you the most about ADD?

24. Are there any advantages to having ADD?

25. Do you take any medications for your ADD?

_____Yes

_____No

26. If Question 26 is "yes," what medications do you now take?

27. If you take medications for ADD, do you think they help? If so, how do they help?

28. Is there anything that I have not asked you that is important for moms with ADD to know?

THANK YOU!

Note: if you want to learn what I found out from my research, interviews, and questionnaires about mothers with ADD, be sure to read my book, *Moms with ADD* (Taylor Publishing, 2000).

The biggest problem I have with the Internet is that I become so mesmerized by it that I have trouble stopping myself and shutting the computer down. I go from link to link to link, thinking I need "just one more" piece of information. It is really quite seductive!

4. Writing for the Internet

Some writers make all or a substantial proportion of their income writing material for Web sites. I was offered a full-time job writing medical how-to information (which would have been double-checked by a physician) for a medical Web site. The work would have been done from my home, where I would have e-mailed it to the editor. It sounded good, but I turned it down because I make more money as a freelance writer than they offered me. Also, I was reticent about losing my autonomy and the freedom to walk away from a job.

There is so much to say about writing for the Web, and I can't possibly say it all. Fortunately, someone else already has. *Writing for the Web* by Crawford Kilian (Self-Counsel Press, 1999) is an excellent book that I highly recommend. If you are considering writing for someone's Web site or creating your own site, you need this book.

Part 4
Taking Care of Business — From a Writer's Perspective

CHAPTER 13

Starting Your Business

Freelance writing is fun and life enhancing and many other positive things. But assuming that you want to make money from your free-lancing, it is also a business. As a result, there are basic business deci-sions you'll need to make, such as choosing a name for your business (although most writers use their own name), creating professional let-terhead, obtaining the needed tools, and so forth. Depending on the laws in your area, you may also need to obtain a business license, al-though many freelancers do not have such licenses. This chapter covers the basics of setting up a freelance writing business.

1. Choose a name

You can choose to use your own name or you may wish to have a busi-ness name (e.g., Creative Enterprises). Your local business authority can tell you what is required to register a business name. Your bank can help you set up a checking account under that name as well.

I use my own name for all my books and I use a business name for other purposes. For example, I have written several adoption books and on various occasions decided to sell them myself to specific markets. I called my business "Adoption Advocates Press" because I was selling adoption books. I registered the name with my city and county, advertised the name in the local newspaper, opened a checking account under that name, and I was ready.

Although you could choose to incorporate, most writers operate as sole proprietorships, which means the business is owned entirely by you and is not a corporate entity.

Unless you plan to create or extend your business into a public relations firm or sell specialized books as I sometimes do, I see no advantage in establishing your business under any name other than your own. Most prospective customers will quickly realize that you are a one-person operation. Calling yourself something like International Communications is unlikely to generate more assignments for you.

2. Select your equipment: Tools of the writing trade

There are certain basic tools of the trade that every successful freelance writer needs. These are tools that enable you to effectively research and produce your work and also communicate with others.

2.1 Computer-related tools

In this section I'll cover the basics about the devices you need in a computerized office. Of course, the main item you need is a computer itself.

2.1.a A computer

The days of pounding out copy on an old typewriter are over for the writer who expects to earn a decent living. Face it: your competition uses computers and word-processing programs, and you should too.

I am not going to give you advice about what kind of computer or word-processing program to buy. Models and prices change too quickly and I'm not an expert in the field. I use an IBM-compatible computer with Microsoft Windows software and a Hewlett Packard laser printer. However, I acknowledge that other computers and programs work very well. Most of my customers prefer an IBM format rather than a Macintosh computer; however, it is possible to save Macintosh data into an IBM format.

Some writers use portable computers. They are good devices if you need to travel a lot, which I don't.

You will definitely need a hard drive on your computer to hold plenty of material. The hard drive is usually built into the computer and you never see it. You will probably want one or more "floppy" drives, which aren't floppy at all, but it's what they're called. Floppy disks are useful if you want to transfer information from one computer to another.

2.1.b A printer

Laser printers are fast and produce beautiful clean copy. I use a laser printer, so I may be biased! Inkjet printers also do a good job. Color printers are available, although I have never felt the need to produce any document in color. You might want to buy a printer that can double as a copier. Check around and do plenty of comparison-shopping. You may find good deals over the Internet or by mail order.

2.1.c Zip your drive

You should have at least one "floppy" drive in addition to the hard drive on your computer. But another great addition to your computer is a zip drive, which you can use to back up the work you've done on your hard drive.

The disks you use in this drive are larger than floppy disks, and the amount of material they hold varies. Mine holds 100 megabytes but there are newer versions that hold 250 megabytes or more. This is enough room for an entire book manuscript and more.

I use my zip drive disks to archive material, taking old files off the hard drive so they don't clutter it up. These old files are valuable enough that I don't want to delete them entirely, but I don't need them too often. Truth be told, I may *never* need some of these old files again. But I like them — so they stay for now.

2.1.d CD-ROM drive

Although not a mandatory requirement at this time, you may wish to purchase a CD-ROM drive. Certainly if you are setting up your new office and buying a computer, you should get one. With a CD-ROM drive, your computer can read special compact disks that can contain enormous amounts of information, such as an entire encyclopedia or the telephone numbers of people across the country.

2.1.e A scanner

Some writers choose to buy a computer scanner, although such a device is certainly not a "must" for most freelance writers. They may wish to scan typewritten information so that it is available on disk. I have used a scanner to scan in a book that I was updating after several years.

The scanner converts the material on the printed page to an image. This image can then be processed using optical character recognition (OCR) software and subsequently saved as a file to a disk.

freelance facts

Scanning the pages on your horizon

It would be nice, wouldn't it, if you could take a portable scanner with you to the library? Let's say you find one or more perfect journal or magazine article, but the library won't allow you to check the material out. Imagine if, instead of standing in line at the photocopy machine and feeding in too many dimes, you could just run your handheld scanner across the printed page and save the pages you want to disk. (I am assuming in this case that such scanning would be done for research purposes only.)

Actually, this is possible now if you have a laptop computer (costing about $1,000) that you can hook up to a portable scanner. I have seriously considered buying a laptop computer for this use only. But the price is still painfully too high.

However, just as I am wrapping up the manuscript for this book, I discovered a new device called the "C Pen 200," created by a Swedish company and available through distributors in North America. It costs $200 and I have ordered one for myself. This pen-like device apparently allows you to scan up to 100 pages of text. It stores the pages in its tiny computer, and you can download them to your PC later on. (The C Pen 200 is not compatible with Macs.) There is also a more upscale version of the pen for about $400, which can supposedly save more than ten times what the C Pen 200 can save. For more information on this new high-tech device, go to this Web site: www.cpen.com.

Since I haven't had the opportunity yet to try the C Pen 200, I can't report on its pros and cons but I can state that I am very hopeful this device may save me a lot of time and money.

2.1.f Playing mouse and cat

Years ago I used only my keyboard to type. But once I started using Windows software, I needed to start using a mouse. This is because Windows uses a lot of icons that you need to "point and click" at, and you do this using a mouse.

A mouse is a device that is smaller than the palm of an adult's hand. With it you can move the cursor on your computer screen. It also allows you to mark blocks of text to be moved or deleted, to pull down menus, and to accomplish many other tasks.

Your mouse will also need a mouse pad to rest on, rather than keeping it directly on your desk. This will help keep your mouse clean. I recently learned that there is an optical mouse which does not require cleaning, and I plan to get one.

I wasn't very good with the mouse at first, and my husband told me I needed lots of "mousercize." Now I'm a pro. My husband uses a touchpad, also known as a "cat," but this device is far too sensitive for me. Keep in mind that cats are now built in to many laptop computers. You may need some "catercize" if you find the cat a little awkward at first.

2.1.g Software

(a) *Word processing.* You will need a word-processing program to do your work. There are a variety of good products available, but keep in mind what most editors want. From my experience, many editors prefer Microsoft Word and they also use Windows-based software as their basic operating system.

(b) *Anti-virus.* You may wish to buy anti-virus software from Norton or another software company. Why? Because there are some annoying or bad people out there whose meaning and purpose in life seems to be to cause havoc and destruction. They may find you at random. Or they may find you because of your use of the Internet:

When you use the Internet, you leave a trail behind you (called, inexplicably, "cookies"), and people who understand how to use this technology can follow you back and send you unsolicited e-mail. Most of the time, if you open these e-mails, they are pornography and so you delete them. (Unless you want pornography. If you do, you will just love the Internet.)

Occasionally, however, if you open the file, it will send a virus out to destroy all your other files. The best idea is not to open mail that looks fishy, although the bad guys are getting pretty tricky about making their "spam" (i.e., unwanted mail) look like it's on the level — until you open it up.

(c) *Disk and hard drive management.* I like Norton software, which can find potential problems in my disks and correct them. Also, if you are like me and work on several different projects at once, making many different changes, your hard drive can become very "fragmented," and you may need software to defragment your hard drive. Fragmented drives are slower, and defragmenting your disk can actually free up space without deleting any files.

When your computer saves a file, it doesn't always save it near the other blocks for the same file. If your drive becomes very fragmented, when you call up a file your computer has to go all over the place to find the blocks that go together. This slows down the speed of your computer.

If you defragment your hard drive, the computer will place like blocks with like blocks and this will speed up operations considerably. I periodically check the fragmentation percentage. If it is below 90%, I order a defragmentation.

(d) *Invoicing and accounting.* You may wish to purchase an invoice program, although do be careful. I bought one program, which I will not identify, that I could never use because it was so fancy I couldn't figure it out. I send maybe 20 invoices at most per year, and this program was designed for someone who sends out hundreds. So now I merely type my invoices in Word. I still get paid, even without fancy invoices, and that's the main thing!

There are many other programs that may be useful to a writer, such as Quicken to track your income and expenses. It's impossible to cover them all and more are created every day. Check your local computer store.

2.1.h A modem

A modem is a device that links your computer to your telephone and enables you to communicate with other computers through your Internet service provider (see chapter 12 for more on ISPs). I consider the modem to be a necessity for every serious writer. Why? Because in an increasing number of cases, editors and clients demand transmission of the material to their own e-mail addresses. They also often like to send e-mail to writers, and most editors assume that professional writers have the capability to receive and send electronic mail. To do that, you need your modem and the service that enables you to use e-mail.

Some modems are inside the computer while others are external. Both formats have their pros and cons, and it's really up to you to decide which is best for your situation.

2.2 Other important "hardware" items

Not every piece of equipment that you need is computerized — although more and more items contain some aspect of a computer. This section covers the fax machine, the answering machine or answering service, the telephone, the copier, the camera, and the tape recorder. You probably will not need all of these; for example, you may do fine without a copier or a camera.

2.2.a A fax machine

My sales went up a great deal after I bought my first fax machine a few years ago. Why? Because I can send or receive an instant response. I have presented an idea to an editor who was a total stranger to me, been told to fax some clips, and been assigned a story within two hours. Of course it doesn't always work out this way. But it can.

Put your fax number on your letterhead, underneath your regular telephone number. It makes you appear very serious about your work. (And you are, aren't you?)

When you use a fax, keep the following points in mind:

- Don't fax long documents without permission. It can be very annoying to the recipient to have his or her fax machine tied up.

- If you are sending only a part of a manuscript or article, let the recipient know, so he or she doesn't think the rest of it got lost somewhere. You can either mention this on a cover sheet or jot a note on the first page you send.

- If you can't afford or don't want to buy a fax machine, your modem may allow your computer to act like a fax machine.

The best aspect of the fax machine is that it speeds up transmission and you don't have to depend on "snail mail," a term some people use to refer to the postal service.

My fax machine doubles as an answering machine; it can differentiate between the loud screechy tone of an incoming fax and the sound of a voice. If it's a fax, the machine switches to fax mode. If it's a person, it turns on the answering machine tape. If the person calling wants to send a fax after leaving a message, he or she can start the fax transmission and the machine will switch to fax mode.

I receive faxes from my editors, who send me everything from names of people they want interviewed to actual contracts. I have also received unsolicited story ideas, or even assignments people want me to do, via my fax line.

Some people have fax machines that use regular white bond paper. I still use thermal paper because a lot of the faxes I receive are not information that I need to keep for long. If I think the fax is important, I will photocopy it.

There are also fax machines that can photocopy documents. My fax machine can make copies, but they are made on thermal paper and look pretty bad. I use my copier for most copies.

2.2.b An answering machine or service

If you already have an answering machine, you can use it for your business. But get rid of the kiddie messages and stupid jingles. Keep your message brief and to the point. Answering machines can capture important assignments you would otherwise miss out on, messages from editors, and so on.

Your telephone company may provide an answering service. I use a service called "Memory Call," offered by Southern Bell. I prerecorded a message and the telephone company plays it if I am unavailable or can't or don't want to answer the telephone. When I pick up the telephone, the sound of the dial tone lets me know if I have messages. I have selected the stuttering option, which sounds like a drunken dial tone. (This very different dial tone prevents me from using my modem, which is an encouragement for me to retrieve my messages.)

One element that I particularly like about this service is that if I am already on the telephone and someone is trying to call me on the same line, instead of receiving a busy signal, they are switched to the prerecorded message. I can't tell you how many important calls I would have missed out on without this service, but I know there would have been some. Why? Because many people are easily frustrated; if they can't get you the first or second time, they give up altogether. And you might never know that they were trying to reach you at all.

Sometimes you may choose not to answer the telephone while you are home and working. The telephone can be a terrible distraction for a writer facing a deadline, and you may decide that you will only pick up if it's an emergency. Make sure your friends and family know that the telephone will be answered with the message that you have chosen, so that they won't hurriedly hang up if they should call to leave a message.

2.2.c A telephone

It's obvious that you need a telephone, but I have a few comments to make on this very important tool. It's okay to use your home telephone as your work one, but get an extension so you can talk in your office area, away from the family and with a little more privacy. Some writers prefer to pay for a separate line so editors won't get a busy signal or be shunted to the answering service because a teenager is talking to a friend.

There are a variety of telephone services available, all with an array of choices, too many to describe in this book. Compare and contrast offerings and choose the best one for you.

One telephone service that can be helpful, albeit pricey, is Caller ID. I have Caller ID and I like it. I originally signed up because my teenage children wanted to be able to see which of their friends was calling. But now I can see right away if an important client is calling me — in which case I drop everything and pick up the telephone. If, on the other hand, it's someone I don't want to talk to (a rarity, but it happens), then I can ignore that person until I feel like returning the call.

The telephone instrument itself merits mention. Many telephones offer automatic redial so if the line you just called was busy, you need only press one button to make the call again. This call is especially useful in calling doctor's offices and government agencies. Another option that you may find useful is the ability to preprogram telephone numbers that you frequently call, so you need only press one digit if you want to connect with a particular person.

You may wish to use a telephone headset so that your hands are free to write things down and you don't get neck or shoulder aches from trying to balance the telephone between your ear and shoulder while doing something else.

2.2.d A copier

Although many writers don't have a photocopying machine, prices are coming down drastically and if you can afford one, you may find it is a good investment. A copier allows you to photocopy your clips (published articles or other materials you have written), interesting magazine articles, and many other documents and avoid a trip to the local copy center. I have a copier because I concentrate on writing books and frequently need to copy articles from journals or pages from books.

Many photocopy machines offer both color and black-and-white printing. My copier can reproduce in color but I don't need this option. I have it only because my husband bought me the machine for Christmas and he was terribly impressed with the color option.

2.2.e A camera

You don't have to be a professional photographer to use a camera. Writers are often in situations where pictures must be taken. Guess who gets to take them? You do!

Generally it is best to shoot color prints because you can get them developed locally and these photos can also be scanned — by you or someone else.

Black-and-white photos can be scanned too. In 1999 I realized that I had only one black-and-white photograph of myself left, and I really liked that picture. An editor needed a photo right away. Did I want to send my one and only photo to the editor who asked for it? The one that I had lost the negative for? Of course not. I scanned the photo, made a computer image of it, and e-mailed the file. We were both happy.

When I need to take a photo, I use a simple camera with auto-focus and auto-everything. I talk to my subject during the photo session (which is usually right after the interview), laugh, kid around, and don't shoot until the person looks at least marginally relaxed. Shoot a whole roll and you'll get at least one good photo in most cases.

Sometimes your interviewees have photos of themselves, which may have been professionally shot. This is good. They may also have their image on a computer file they can provide you. But if you need a photo of your subject on the job or doing something relevant to your book or article, take those pictures yourself if necessary.

Some writers take an introductory course on photography or read books on the subject. Check your local community college and your library to see if these options are available to you.

2.2.f A tape recorder

I have one microcassette recorder to take out on interviews and one standard-sized cassette recorder that is always hooked up to my telephone to tape interviews.

It is essential to tape telephone interviews. No matter how effective you are at taking notes, often there are many distractions.

People on the other end may be giving you complicated information. If you have it on tape, you can listen to the interview later and make sure you get it right.

You can use virtually any type of tape recorder and need only purchase a recorder control device to hook your tape recorder to your telephone line.

One cable of the recorder control device plugs directly into your telephone jack. The other cables from the device plug into your recorder. These devices sell for about $20 and up, and you can buy them at Radio Shack and similar outlets. There are also cassette recorders specifically designed for recording off the telephone. They cost about $50 and come with necessary cables and instructions. Which is better, a microcassette recorder or a larger-sized recorder? I prefer the microcassette recorder for in-person interviews because it fits easily into a purse or briefcase and is unobtrusive and nonthreatening. The downside of microcassettes is that they are easy to lose because they are so tiny, so be careful. I like the bigger recorder for at-home interviews because I want something more substantial in my home office. However, this is a personal preference and you may have a different view.

One recommendation: when you are interviewing someone over the telephone, be sure to tell the person that you are taping him or her at the beginning of the interview and explain that you want your quotations to be accurate. Most people are terrified of being misquoted and appreciate being taped. See chapter 11 for more on using a tape recorder for interviews.

Whatever recorder you use, be sure to label your tapes. If you are interviewing many people for one article or you're working on several articles or a book (or all of the above), it is too easy to become confused about which tape includes which interview. You don't want to waste your time listening to tapes over and over to find the right one.

This is the voice of experience here — don't make this mistake that I have made myself in the past. It causes a lot of frustration! Should you tape over old tapes? That's a judgment call. When you have completed an interview and the project has been published, it is probably safe to tape over, although some people save their tapes for years. If you do tape over a previous interview, be sure to relabel your tape.

Take notes even when you are taping a person. For one thing, you can jot down thoughts or questions as they occur to you without interrupting the flow of the interviewee's thoughts. Another reason is there are those horrible occasions when your tape machine runs out of tape and you don't realize it or it fails altogether. So take notes as an emergency backup.

2.3 Your office environment

The area that you work in is important, and in the next section I discuss items that are generally found in the office, including your desk, lighting, and ergonomic devices you may use to avoid repetitive strain injuries.

2.3.a A desk

You can buy a computer desk at many office supply stores. Get a desk that is not too low or too high. Consider where your computer will be situated and where you will be in relation to your desk when sitting in your chair. Your arms should be held loosely at your sides, not straining upward or down, so your hands settle easily on the computer keyboard. For some reason, many people put their computers too high up and risk neck strain. Lower is better.

2.3.b Lighting

Make sure that you have good lighting in your home office. As a writer, you use your eyes constantly and you must avoid eyestrain. Lighting should be neither too dim nor too bright, and you must gauge what is best for you. You may wish to use adjustable lamps. I don't recommend fluorescent lighting because its buzzing and flickering can be very annoying.

2.3.c Ergonomic devices

There are numerous devices to make your office better suited to your body and help you avoid such ailments as carpal tunnel syndrome, which can occur in the hands and arms and is exacerbated by a lot of typing. Ask at your local computer store about equipment that can make typing less of a pain.

Other parts of the body, such as the neck, can also be strained. To limit neck strain, I recommend you purchase an inexpensive copyholder. When you are typing information printed on papers, this device will let you see your copy at eye level without craning your neck. (I also use the copyholder to hold onto items that I must respond to soon.)

As mentioned in section **2.2.c** above, you can purchase a telephone headset that helps you avoid straining your neck as you cradle the telephone between ear and shoulder. It is also easier to take notes this way.

Get a comfortable chair, preferably with arms, and be sure your back is well supported.

No matter how ergonomically balanced your office is, you should take periodic breaks and at least walk around the room. Don't stare intently at the computer screen for hours. You'll hurt your eyes. Instead, glance away periodically — at least every 30 minutes or so.

2.3.d Reference books

Reference books are a valuable tool for every writer. A good college-level dictionary is essential and can be purchased from your local bookstore. I use *Merriam Webster's Collegiate Dictionary* in the paperback edition.

Another important reference is *Roget's International Thesaurus*. This source is useful for those times when you don't want to use the same word twice or you can't quite think of the right word. If you draw a complete blank, you can page through the index and seek a similar word.

What about quotations? They can make your prose sparkle. People have made wonderful remarks; a pithy quote may be just what you need to round out your article. One source I use for quotes is the *International Thesaurus of Quotations*.

You may also find sources from your past. I still have some of my literature textbooks from long-ago college days, and every once in awhile I find something useful to use in my work. Tailor your reference library to your particular needs.

3. Your professional image

You need to project a professional image to those who don't know you — and even to those editors and clients you've worked with before. Key among these items is the letterhead you use. Business cards are also important, and some writers create brochures that they can hand out to prospective clients.

If you have a brochure, you can use the same text and graphics in a Web site that promotes you and your work.

3.1 Letterhead

Letterhead is essential when you are starting out. It creates a sense of professionalism, permanency, and seriousness. You absolutely must use letterhead if you plan to be a profit-making writer.

You need not spend a lot of money creating a gorgeous masterpiece, nor should you choose shocking pink or any Day-Glo color for your paper. Use either white or off-white paper and black ink. (Colored ink costs more and is unlikely to net you any more sales.)

I consider my letterhead even more essential than my fax machine, which I value highly. My sales went up dramatically shortly after I created letterhead. I know I didn't become a better writer in just two weeks, especially since I was sending out the same ideas, written up the same way. The only difference was the letterhead.

Keep your letterhead simple, with your name, address, telephone number, fax number, and e-mail address. If you must, you can add professional affiliations, but they generally don't enhance appearance. Don't put "freelance writer" or "writer" under your name. Tell the person you're a writer in the text of your letter.

Avoid pasting graphics and symbols all over your letterhead. If it is too fancy and/or cluttered, this letterhead will turn people off and could impair the professional image you wish to convey. You can ask a printer to help you design your letterhead or you can design it yourself.

I don't buy letterhead anymore. Instead, I have my letterhead template on disk. When I want to type a letter, I call up that template. Then the whole document, letterhead and letter, is printed out on one pass through my laser printer. I use white copy paper.

3.2 Business cards

Many writers consider business cards to be essential. Most of my work is done through telephone interviews, so I have limited use for business cards, but if you do in-person interviews, people expect you to have cards. They are an inexpensive investment.

Again, forget the fancy stuff. Your name, address, telephone number, fax number, and e-mail address (and Web site, if you have one) are enough information to include on a card.

Don't do what I did with my first business cards. I said I was a "freelance writer, ghostwriter, and collaborator." My husband said the "collaborator" made me sound like a World War II spy, and not on the side of the good guys. I soon dropped the collaborator label.

3.3 Brochures

Some writers create flyers or brochures with their photograph on the cover and a list of the types of work they do inside. You may want to explore this option once you have some experience under your belt.

I don't consider advertising brochures to be important unless most of your business is in the field of public relations or corporate communications. Writers who do use brochures say that they are important to their success.

4. Organizing yourself

Sometimes things can get confusing when you're working on several different jobs. For this reason, you need to get organized. The items discussed next will help you do that. There are many more organizing materials — these are only the basics.

4.1 Your calendar

Whether you buy a huge calendar to hang up on the wall or a desk-size calendar, you will need to record your appointments, due dates, and other important information. Some people put this information on their computer. If an upcoming interview is really important, I also annotate it a few days ahead of time. (I also have been known to leave myself notes on the refrigerator!)

Many writers swear by their office organizers, voluminous books containing telephone numbers, a calendar, and assorted other data. I prefer an office calendar that provides one page for every day. I write down all my appointments, jot myself reminders, note my deadlines, and so forth. I would be lost without it.

4.2 A file cabinet

You'll eventually need a file cabinet to keep your published clips and other paraphernalia, so buy at least one. You can store your materials in boxes, but then your pets could jump on them, kids could spill things on them, and other disasters could happen. It is better if this material is in a safe place away from prying eyes and sticky fingers.

4.3 Get insured

Every writer intent on making a profit should consider taking out home and business insurance. Many insurance companies offer plans that insure your computer and other expensive pieces of equipment for a fairly nominal fee.

You might think you should forego insurance since you are a small-business person. I'm glad I did not. Several years ago, a bolt of lightning shot through my telephone line into my modem and then into my turned-off computer, destroying it forever, including everything on the hard drive. (Disasters like this are also a good argument for backing up your files.) I had surge protection on my line, but this was a direct hit. My hard drive fried and died.

My insurance covered the full replacement cost of the computer — less a small deductible — and was well worth the low premium I had paid for it. I did, however, have to obtain a letter from the company that sold me the computer, attesting that lightning strikes can destroy a built-in modem.

CHAPTER 14

Proper Planning and Goal Setting: Should You Quit Your Day Job?

Now that you know the basics of starting a business, you're aware of what tools you need, you know who you're going to write for and what you want to write about, and you have begun to master the writer's mindset, should you go ahead and quit your job and become a rich and famous author, maybe in a few weeks? Well, hold on — not so fast.

First, it is important to understand that it's rare for writers to become rich overnight. You need time to build up your knowledge and experience, start your marketing, and develop a customer base. This chapter provides tools to help you analyze if you are ready to take the full-time plunge, tools that can be used for years after you become a full-time freelancer.

Thinking of quitting your day job? Ask yourself these questions:

(a) Do I know what my monthly financial obligations are, such as rent or house payment, car payment, utility bills?

(b) How much cash do I have? How much can I obtain by selling stock, borrowing from someone, or by other means?

(c) Do other people in the family depend on my income? If I brought in no money for several months, would we all starve?

(d) Am I considering problems that could come up and that cost money, such as home repairs that can't be delayed? (You can never think of everything, but you should know if the roof on your house is ready to fall apart.)

(e) Do other people in the family depend on my time providing help with algebra homework, cooking, and other tasks? If so, can someone else pinch-hit?

(f) What additional equipment do I need to start my freelance business? How much does it cost?

1. When should you quit your day job?

To answer this question, you must consider many aspects of your own life. For example, do you have enough money saved to support yourself and your family? What if another family member who is now employed were laid off? Would you then still have adequate financial resources?

Keep in mind that your business will cost you dollars, primarily in overhead expenses. Even if you already own a computer, printer, and reams of paper, there will be expenses. Costs for computer disks, pens, and telephone expenses add up fast.

Also keep in mind that you may not receive payment for a job until a month or more after you complete it. Let's say that you turn in your assigned cover story today. The payment isn't going to arrive tomorrow. After you submit the manuscript, the editor has to read it, ask you any questions that still need to be answered, edit it, and then decide to accept it. As a result, it will usually be at least 30 days, and often longer, before that check is really in the mail to you.

> Writing revenues are often sporadic. You may receive a large check this week and then nothing for four weeks. You should have or learn good budgeting skills and know how to s-t-r-e-t-c-h a paycheck, at least in the early part of your writing career.

1.1 Creating a cash flow projection

You should do a simple cash flow projection before you bail out of your current position. I have created a simple one for you to review (see Sample 9), based on the first four months of business for a fictitious writer. The chart shows the writer's existing cash savings, revenues coming in, and business expenses. These are all estimates, and I made no attempt to create realistic numbers. When you create your own cash flow projection, base your numbers on prices of items such as paper, pens, and computer equipment in your area.

As you can see in the chart, the writer starts Month 1 with no freelance cash because it's a new business. But she does have some money: $8,000. Maybe she's saved this amount because she's been planning to go freelance for a long time. Or maybe she won the lottery.

Go down the column for the first month and look at the expenses the writer has projected: postage at $35, telephone at $150, and so forth. Because there is no incoming revenue, she must deduct her expenses from the $8,000 in savings. That leaves a balance of $5,565.

Month 2 starts off with the $5,565 cash from the end of the last column. There are still no checks for work done, so the "Revenues" column stays at zero. After deducting the expenses estimated for the second month, total cash will be down to $5,425.

In the third month, a check for $1,500 arrives. This is added to the $5,425 in cash, which brings the total to $6,925. Of course, there still are some expenses, and deducting them leaves $6,702 in cash.

Month 4 brings a check for $1,626 — and yes, writers do receive checks in odd amounts. It could include reimbursement for telephone

Cash Flow Projection

CASH FLOW PROJECTION OVER FOUR MONTHS

Cash in	Month 1	Month 2	Month 3	Month 4
Cash	$0	$5,565	$5,425	$6,702
Savings	8,000	0	0	0
Revenues	0	0	1,500	1,626
Total Cash	$8,000	$5,565	$6,925	$8,328
Expenses				
Postage	$35	$40	$40	$35
Telephone	150	100	127	200
Office Supplies	250	0	56	77
Equipment	2,000	0	0	0
Total Expenses	$2,435	$140	$223	$312
Cash Balance	$5,565	$5,425	$6,702	$8,016

expenses. We take the beginning cash balance of $6,702, add the check to that, and come up with $8,328. Then we subtract expenses and come up with $8,016. If we wanted to do a Month 5, we would start the column with the $8,016.

On the down side, this $8,016 is only $16 more than the writer had at the beginning: remember, there was $8,000 in the bank when she started. But on the plus side, she knows she has received more assignments and will earn more and bigger checks. And she also knows that it takes more than four months to become self-supporting in a new career field. So all in all, our writer is quite satisfied with her projections.

Please note, however, that this projection includes revenues and expenses for the business only. It does not cover living expenses such as food and shelter. You may wish to include these necessities in your cash flow budget. After all, we writers need sustenance for our bodies as well as our souls.

1.2 Creating an earnings plan

Another tool to help you decide whether you're ready to take the freelance plunge is the earnings plan. Talent alone isn't enough to lead you to success as an entrepreneurial writer. To be a profit-making writer, you need to plan how much money you want to make and how you are going to get it. This involves some hard thinking and serious goal setting.

An earnings plan can be used in several different ways. First, it can be used as a prospective plan in which you anticipate how much you need to earn each month to reach your goal. Once you know what income you need, consider how much you (realistically) expect to make in one year: $10,000, $20,000, $50,000? Keep in mind that you must also cover your overhead expenses (adding at least 20% to your financial goal). Divide your desired annual earnings by 12 to calculate how much you need to earn per month. You may not know how much you *can* earn, but estimate to the best of your ability how much you *need*.

Adjust your monthly and annual goals if necessary to reflect reality. For example, if you planned on earning $3,000 per month and you haven't made over $2,000 — with no increase in work on the horizon — you may want to drop your monthly target by $1,000.

An earnings plan can also be used for retrospective review — you can look back over the past six months or year and figure out how you did compared to how you think you should have done, and adjust your plan for next year accordingly.

Be realistic. You're not going to make $100,000 in your first year as an entrepreneurial writer. If you're planning to work full time, plan on earning a living wage. The premise of this is that with talent, aggressiveness, and good planning, you can make a living wage.

Sample 10 shows an earnings plan for a freelance writer. He has set himself a goal of earning $2,500 per month so he can reach gross revenues of $30,000 for the year.

In January, the writer anticipates receiving $1,000. This is good, but it is $1,500 less than his goal of $2,500. This shortfall can be represented on the earnings plan with the notation, in the third column, -1500. Some people put the number in parentheses when they are "in the red," which would look like this: (1,500).

In February, the writer thinks he will have a great month and earn $4,000. That means his total anticipated revenues (the middle column) are $5,000. Since he wanted to earn $2,500 per month, he will be right on target (if his projections turn out to be correct) because that $4,000 will cover the $1,500 he was short in January and will also meet his $2,500 monthly goal for February.

Follow the projected ups and downs through the months. At the end of the year, we see that the writer expects to gross $31,024. This is above his target gross earnings of $30,000 by $1,024, so if he does earn this much, he'll be ahead of his plan.

When you set up your first earnings plan, you might want to have it run for a shorter period, say three months or six months, until you achieve some accuracy in projecting earnings. Because freelance earnings can be sporadic, and because many writers can have a terrible month or two, especially during the first few years in the business, you may also wish to avoid comparing actual earnings to projected earnings every single month. Instead, wait until you have actual earnings for at least four, six, or twelve months and then make a new chart that compares actual earnings with the projected earnings. You could also make a three-columned chart to show what you needed to make each month to reach your goal, what you thought you would make each month, and what you did make each month. More data will give you a more valid idea of how well you are doing compared to how you thought you would be doing.

Earnings Plan

Goal: $30,000 gross sales per year, or $2,500/month

Month	Received ($)	Total Revenues ($)	+/- Your Goal ($)
JAN	1,000	1,000	-1,500
FEB	4,000	5,000	+0
MAR	2,000	7,000	-500
APR	3,200	10,200	+200
MAY	100	11,700	-800
JUNE	670	12,370	-2,630
JULY	2,100	14,470	-3,030
AUG	3,100	17,570	-2,430
SEPT	2,500	20,070	-2,430
OCT	2,476	22,546	-2,454
NOV	4,100	26,646	-854
DEC	4,378	31,024	+1,024

After you have earned some money over six months to a year, then you can rethink your goals based on actual information and decide whether you have set your sights too high or too low. After you have been in business for at least a year, you will have a better feel for what your earnings goals can realistically be. As you gain more years of experience, this knowledge will provide you with still more data, and you will become even better at predicting earnings. However, all writers, no matter what their level of experience, need to make periodic reviews of how they're doing compared to how they think they should be doing.

How can you use the earnings plan? If you find you are not doing as well as you had hoped, you can ratchet up the number of queries you're sending out and market yourself more aggressively. If you are doing better than you anticipated, then you can turn down jobs that are marginal and accept only the most lucrative and interesting jobs. And you can adjust your earnings plan if it needs to be changed, either upward (hopefully!) or downward.

To avoid discouragement, don't set your goal so high that you can never succeed. If you find that your earnings are very low month after a few months, you can adjust your earnings goal downward. But don't be too easy on yourself either.

1.3 Set milestones

A milestone refers to a goal or series of goals that you plan to complete by certain dates. One problem many writers have is juggling many projects or even figuring out how to do one major project.

To avoid becoming overwhelmed, I recommend that you periodically create milestones. When a project is big, when you have many projects, or both, break down the big project into smaller increments and the many projects into goals.

First, write down the tasks that you need to perform for each job. For example, for Job A you may need to identify five people to interview and then interview them, do some library and/or online research, and then write the article. Let's say you have three weeks to do this job. You must assign a portion of the time available to do each task. Don't leave the most time-consuming tasks until the last week.

You may have other assignments on the go as well. For Job B, you have already done the research and interviewing and you need to sit down and write the article. This article is due in one week. For Job C, you have written a first draft but you need to review it one more time. The article is due in two weeks.

Once you know what needs to be done to complete each assignment on time, you can make up a daily schedule. Each morning, write down a list of things you must do to achieve your daily goal. After each task has been completed, you can check it off and feel very proud of yourself (see Sample 11).

As you move further into a project, you can become more specific. For example, you may identify Jane Brown and John Doe as people you must interview. Set weeks during which you'd like to interview them. Allow plenty of time because Jane and John may be on vacation, sick, or just too busy to talk to you when you want to talk to them.

Post your three-week plan on a bulletin board or wall or clipboard so you can periodically remind yourself where you are on the project.

> If you are writing a book, it is better to create a work plan that encompasses months rather than weeks.

1.3.a Number of pages or number of hours goals

Some writers set a goal of a certain number of pages or words to write each day, while others set a goal of a number of hours to work. Set a goal that will stretch you but won't give you a nervous breakdown. Then give yourself a little reward when you're done. Go watch a favorite television show, go for a walk, or just mellow out.

1.3.b Marketing goals

You may set a marketing goal for yourself; for example, sending out a certain number of queries within a time period. Some writers set a goal for the number of queries or proposals to send out per week. Maybe it's six, maybe it's ten. Set a goal that is reasonable for you, but make it more than one query per week. (Some writers routinely send out five to ten queries each week.)

If you are sending out many queries, you can track them on a simple form you create for this purpose (see Sample 12). You can also keep track of queries on a computer spreadsheet or database. Keep a copy of each query letter as well.

Three-Week Plan

	Job A	Job B	Job C
	NEW JOB	**ONGOING JOB**	**ONGOING JOB**
Week 1	Goal: 5 interviews	Write 1st draft	Rev. draft
	Library research	Write final art.	Call ed.
	Online research		
	Networking		
	Setting up interviews		
Week 2	Finish setting up interview		Write final
	Start interviewing		
	Wrap up library research		
	Wrap up online research		
Week 3	Finish all research		
	Write first draft		
	Write final		

Query Tracking Form

Magazine Queries, June 20—

Market	Idea	Query Sent	Result
Markets Today	Computer how-to	4/15	Assignment due 7/15
Florida Armadillo	Mating habits	5/25	Rejected
Aging North Americans	Profile/Jane X	5/25	Assignment due 6/30
Medical Payments	Electronic billing	5/15	No word yet

On the sample form, you can see that a query was sent to *Markets Today* on April 15 with an idea to write a computer how-to article. The result was an assignment, due on July 15.

On May 25 the writer sent a query to *Florida Armadillo* (these are not real magazines — at least, not to my knowledge) for an article about the mating habits of the armadillo. This was quickly rejected on June 4. (When you receive a rejection, you can decide to rethink and reslant the query or you may decide to send the exact same idea to another publication — be sure to change the editor's name and address on your query letter, of course.)

Also on May 25, a proposal to write a profile of Jane X was sent to *Aging North Americans*. The magazine loved the idea and assigned the article, due June 30. Lastly, the writer — clearly someone with eclectic interests — sent an idea to *Medical Payments* for an article on electronic billing. She hasn't heard yet if they are interested.

The sample tracking form contains columns listing the specific market (publication), the idea, the date the query went out, and the end result. You can change the order of the categories if you wish, putting the idea first and the publication second if that works better for you.

Time is money. Try to save as much time as possible.

- Sort the mail into piles of bills, junk, checks, etc. Throw out the mail you don't need.

- Deposit the checks today or no later than tomorrow to improve your financial position.

- Prioritize the action items that you identify among your mail. For example, a client may have written with a question that needs a written reply. Decide how urgent it is to answer, but don't delay longer than a few days.

- Make lists. To-do lists are good. You can also make lists of possible future ideas, lists of questions to ask interviewees, and a myriad of other lists.

- Keep the papers and supplies you need nearby. If you have a project that is not due for months and you don't need to work on it now, file it away.

2. Part time or full time?

Now we're back to the original question of this chapter: Should you quit your day job and become a freelance writer?

You may wish to keep your day job and write part time. However, one potential difficulty with this plan is that if you're working on a piece that requires interviews, most interviewees are only available during the day, which is when you are probably working outside your home. It is not a great idea to use the boss's telephone to call up and interview people for magazine articles you're supposed to be doing on your own time. It could certainly get you fired.

On the other hand, you can write queries in your spare time. There are many types of articles that you can write after the hours of your day job — the personal experience piece, the general information article, the editorial, and, often, the how-to article.

It is also true that many interviewees will agree, and even prefer, to be interviewed during the evening or on the weekend. Away from daytime distractions, they are better able to concentrate on your questions.

When you decide to take the plunge and leave your full-time job for a full-time writing business, it can be scary. You'll be motivated to succeed, but fear can sometimes freeze people up.

The best course of action is to do some analysis and create a plan ahead of time. That way you can hit the ground running with good ideas for what you can write about, who you can write for, approximately how much revenue you anticipate receiving, and what your estimated costs will be. If you make such a plan before you quit your day job, you'll be ahead of the game and ahead of most writers.

You should consider using the estimating tools described in this chapter: the cash flow projection and the earnings estimate. When you become a more established writer, these tools will still be valuable to you and enable you to decide whether to continue in certain areas or discontinue.

For a long time I had not analyzed a newsletter I published. One day I sat down and took a hard look at the numbers and realized that it was time for a radical change. The newsletter was not bringing in enough money to be profitable. I could take steps to try to make it profitable, stop publishing it, or sell it to someone else. I decided to sell it. But had I not done this analysis, I would not have realized the money drain until it was time to figure out my taxes.

In the next chapter, I'll tell you how to evaluate offers, price jobs, and collect payment for those assignments that will give you favorable cash flow and enough earnings.

CHAPTER 15

Money and Getting Paid

It's great to see your name on a book or an article, and it's wonderful when an editor asks you to do more work. But to stay in business as a freelance writer, most of us need to pay attention to the "bottom line," the amount of dollars we earn. This chapter is about money and includes information about offers and receiving the money you're due.

1. How to evaluate an offer

Let's start with the good stuff. It is exhilarating to receive an offer for your work. It's also a good idea to step back and evaluate the offer; don't rush to accept.

When you receive an offer, whether it is for a project you've lobbied for or it comes out of the blue, it is important to evaluate it carefully, no matter how big or small. Some of the issues to consider include the following:

- How much research will this project need? How much time will it take me?

- How much money is the client offering? Does this include expenses?

- How soon is the project due? Do I have time to do it?

- Do I know anything about the subject already or am I going to start from zero?

- Have I written this type of project before? For example, if the editor wants a personality profile and you've never done one, it doesn't mean that you can't do it — it just means it involves extra learning time.

- Will your work be subject to a lot of review? You need to know this ahead of time. The more people who will look over and critique what you write, the more money you should be paid. A committee of writers is bound to find plenty of changes they think you should make. Sometimes several of your critics may give opposing advice or directions — this has happened to me! — and it will take you time to find the middle ground.

- If you're offered a highly technical job and you feel that it is outside your area of knowledge and expertise, don't be dazzled by the money. Turn it down.

- Who is making the offer? Can your client afford to pay you and does he or she appear to be honorable?

When you're working for a corporation or the government, you expect to receive your weekly or biweekly paycheck. You may be worried about stretching it to meet your bills, but you do know it's coming. Not true when you are a business owner. In your own writing business you're owed money for jobs, but it's your responsibility to make sure you price a job right and that you get paid.

Before we get into the details of pricing a job, it's important for you to keep in mind that a job that pays $200 may be a better deal for you than a job that pays $1,000. Why? Because the job that pays $1,000 may include no expenses and require many hours of work, whereas the job that pays the "mere" $200 may be a simple task for you. It is vital that you take into consideration how many hours a job will take and how hard it is.

In many cases, you won't have much — if any — negotiating room on what you will be paid. But if you are venturing into work for businesses or ghostwriting work, and sometimes in the case of magazine writing, you may be asked how much you charge.

2. Jobs and money

2.1 How to price a job

Often you'll be asked to do a job you've never done before and you must decide how much to charge. So how *do* you decide?

2.1.a Previous experience — yours and others

If you have any writing experience, think about what you have charged before for similar jobs. (If the job was a long time ago, be sure to add more dollars to take that factor into account.)

As well, ask your colleagues what they have charged for similar jobs, especially if they are not in the same geographic location as you and are not competitors. Find out if they generally ask for one flat rate and if they receive reimbursement for expenses. Do they ask for money up front? Do they ask for periodic progress payments?

2.1.b Determine your own profit margin

Despite what your colleagues may receive, you should also determine if this job will be profitable for you. Set an hourly rate that you'd like to earn. Don't make it too low. Writers are more likely to underbid than overbid.

For example, let's say you'd like to earn $40 per hour. Remember, you have overhead expenses to cover and $40 payable to you as an entrepreneur is not the same as $40 payable to you as an employee, where your employer picks up the overhead and pays employee benefits.

Now determine how many hours you think this job will take. Break the job up into segments. If it is a special report, ask for samples of previous special reports so you can see what the job is supposed to look like at completion. Does the client want you to first submit an outline or a rough draft of the project? Or does he or she not want to hear from you until you are close to completion? The more client participation, the longer the job could be, so you need to take this information into account.

Determine how many parts there are to this project and what kind of work will go into it. Perhaps the job will require 10 hours of research and 20 hours of writing, for a total of 30 hours.

This is not the figure you give the client; we're not finished yet! Next, find out if this job includes or does not include expenses you will incur, such as online research and telephone and fax expenses. If it does not, then you should add enough hours to compensate for that lack.

Even if the client will pay an add-on for expenses, you should take a very hard look at the number of hours you've come up with. Why? Because things take longer than we expect them to. Add in a "fudge factor" of at least 25% or more depending on how good you are at pricing jobs. Add 25% at least for a new client and a new kind of job. Sample 13 shows how to price different projects and decide whether to accept or reject them.

A factor to consider when pricing a job is your own level of expertise. If you have written on the topic many times before, your background and knowledge lend extra value to the project. Also, if you have contacts in the field on whom you can rely, these also add value. Should you add on 10% or 20%? Only you can determine how much extra to add on because of your experience level and other unquantifiable factors.

Deciding Whether to Accept a Job

Pricing a New Client

Hourly rate you need	$50
Hours you think job will take	20 hours (*Estimate high)
Expenses? Will publisher pay?	No
If no, anticipated expenses	$500
Total	$1,500
Aggravation factor	10%
You need to receive	$1,650

*In estimating how many hours a job will take, include telephone calls, trips to the library, typing, and just plain thinking.

Deciding To Turn Down a Job

Hourly rate you will need	$40
Hours job will take	30
Client pays expenses?	Yes
You need ($40 x 30)	$1,200
Aggravation/Fun factor (This is a tough client!)	20%
You need total of:	$1,440
Client offers you:	$800

Turn this job down unless you can negotiate for more.

Deciding To Accept a Job

Hourly rate	$30 per hour
Hours/job will take	20 hours
Aggravation factor	0 (You love this client!)
You need ($30 x 20)	$600
Fun factor	20% (i.e., you deduct 20% from price to do this fun job)
You need total of:	$480
Client offers you	$500

Go ahead and do the job.

Should you bill the client at an hourly rate? I avoid it whenever possible because there is a tendency for the client to presume or suspect you may be dragging your feet if you're paid by the hour. But if you're being paid by the job, it's in your own best interests to do the job well and promptly.

2.1.c The aggravation factor

Don't forget to consider the aggravation factor, a term I use to describe how difficult you think a project will be. If this is a client you've worked with before and you know he or she is difficult, then you'll have a higher aggravation factor. If this is a new client, there is an aggravation factor because you don't yet know if you'll be able to work well together. For a new client I add in an aggravation factor of at least 10%.

If I've worked with someone before and we got along well, that client gets a zero aggravation factor. A former client who has given me grief — yet pays enough to compensate — could get any range of aggravation factors.

What else is aggravating? For me, being given a week to do a difficult job and clients who constantly change their minds are aggravating.

You can use the aggravation factor as part of your pricing strategy. Also, if someone offers you a certain amount of money for a job, you can use the aggravation factor to determine if it is going to be worth it.

Figure out what you need to earn times the number of hours you think the job will take. Always overestimate the number of hours. Too many writers tend to think a job will be easier than it turns out to be. Consider whether the client will pay your telephone, fax, and travel expenses. Then, when that total is determined, add on the aggravation factor (or fun factor) to obtain your final price.

2.1.d The fun factor

Another consideration is whether the project appeals to you. You might consider taking on a lower-paying assignment because it has an element of fun. You adore working with the editor, so any assignment with him or her is a plus. Your fun factor could be 10% or more, depending on the project.

Some people may think factoring in fun is silly, but I feel that enjoyability should be taken into account, at least sometimes.

A fun factor is deducted from the price you've calculated because you're willing to take less in order to work on this project. Assign a fun factor to special projects only. A job is fun if I know and like the editor and the subject sounds fascinating. If I am given enough time to do the job at an unhurried pace, that is fun too.

It is important to note, however, that in some, if not many cases, you will still need to turn down projects that are fun. You are in business to make money and not to be entertained.

2.1.e Other sources of information

There are other sources to check for types of fees charged. For example, the *Writer's Market*, published annually, provides general information on how much writers charge for many types of jobs. In addition, it gives ranges of fees paid to writers by various publishers.

Some writers' organizations also give information on fees received by others; for example, if you join the American Society of Journalists & Authors (you need to have some publishing credits to join), they provide information on fees received by other members for various types of jobs. Other writers groups may provide similar information. See the Appendix for a list of groups.

Remember, these figures are not cast in stone! A client may offer you less, but often will offer you more if you appear to be worth it.

2.2 Fees for complicated jobs

If the job requires you to interview many people, take that time into account when you calculate the time needed to do the job. If you transcribe your tapes, take that time into account as well. If your project is subject to review by more than two or three people, be sure to add plenty of extra hours. The more people there are involved in a project, the more difficult it is.

Try hard to delay the discussion of money. The one who brings up a figure first usually loses. Your client may have deep pockets and can make you a very generous offer. After all, you're worth it! On the other hand, he or she is not going to spend extra money if it can be avoided.

What about the job turnaround? If the client needs the job very quickly, say in a week or a month, he or she may be willing to pay more than usual out of desperation.

Why not charge more, since you will have to work harder? If you were working overtime in a supermarket, you'd expect to get paid extra. So why should it be different if you're a writer?

Another factor to consider is how much the client can afford. This can be tough. If the client is business-savvy, he or she will not want to tell you what the limit is; you should ask anyway. "What's your projected budget for this assignment?" is a polite way to find out how much you will be offered.

> What should you do to show your fascination and interest in a project? Ask a lot of questions, describe similar work that you have done, mention contacts who can assist you, and get your client interested in giving you the job.

2.3 The best position: A job you can walk away from

It's ironic but so often true that when you don't especially need jobs, everyone wants you to write for them. It may be more than just happenstance. When you don't need a particular job, then you're not desperate and are more relaxed. This comes across to editors as an aura of confidence and competence, which thus leads them to believe that they need YOU.

What if you really do need the job? Then act as if you are somewhat interested. But remember that you are not going to die if you don't get this job. In fact, you can use those words. What will happen if I don't get this job? Will I die? Will my spouse divorce me? Will everyone I know shun me? Of course not. Keeping this in mind will make it easier for you to present an image of interested — but not desperate.

> In the beginning of your career, you may think there are no jobs you can afford to walk away from. But there probably are. The jobs that will take long hours and pay very little when you could be spending this time marketing to bigger, better publishers — these are the jobs you should turn down.

2.4 When to ask for money up front

When you're offered a lengthy job that will take weeks or months or longer, or if a job pays $2,000 or more, you should always ask for money up front.

This is particularly important when you are beginning your writing business. Many writers have worked hard on projects for which they were never paid. The client wasn't necessarily dishonest. Disasters can happen: clients become ill, companies go out of business. For your protection and security, ask for money up front whenever possible. Call it a retainer, or an advance, or whatever name you feel comfortable with.

How much should you ask for? I'd ask for at least one third of the total job up front, or half if you think you can get it. Beyond that, it's doubtful if the client would agree.

Actually, this up-front money has a good psychological advantage for both you and your client. You have some money in your pocket and you're motivated to do the job. The client has paid you and can expect you to produce results — and has the right to contact you periodically to find out how you're doing.

2.5 Reimbursable expenses

Expenses can be billed on a monthly basis or at the end of the job, whichever is more convenient. When your client is new, he or she may request copies of telephone bills and other receipts as well as an annotated list with your invoice.

What expenses do most clients accept? Telephone and fax charges and overnight mail service fees are usually acceptable expenses. Travel expenses can be included too, if this was agreed upon beforehand.

Some expenses are presumed to be part of your overhead. For example, few clients cover the cost of your diskettes, paper, or postage. Some clients will return diskettes to you for your reuse, but that's not common.

Make sure that you both agree on what kind of expenses are to be covered, no matter who your client is.

Sometimes your client will request an upper limit on expenses; for example, you may bill for up to $200 in telephone expenses and after that you have to pay them yourself. Clients put a cap on expense claims to discourage freelancers from taking advantage of their largesse. As a writer and researcher, you need to make the most efficient use possible of your telephone.

However, if your client suddenly needs you to call someone in Geneva, Switzerland (and this has happened to me!), then you should be able to add on such special expenses.

3. Contracts

The word "contract" really scares a lot of people. Contracts can be full of confusing legal jargon that only lawyers can understand, but they don't have to be.

A contract is an agreement between at least two people. It can be oral or written. In the writing business, it should be written. Many of your clients have their own standard contract forms that they will ask you to sign. Read them over and sign them if they seem fair.

If there's something in a contract that you don't like, cross it out and initial it. It could be a minor clause that everyone ignores anyway, but it might be something that could cost you the job! Remember, though, that you are in this to make a profit and you should not take on jobs that will cost you money with no other benefit in sight.

> When you first contact a possible client, often by letter, he or she may telephone you and tell you to go ahead since your terms are fair. Always ask if the client can send you a note to that effect on company letterhead. If he or she cannot or will not, then you should send a written letter summarizing your understanding of what the client wants you to do, how much you'll receive, and when to send it. This is called "reverse contracting." This tactic has always worked well for me.

A written contract is important because it spells out what is expected of everyone. If there is any disagreement later on, you have the contract to refer to. With no contract, your client could say he or she wanted 20,000 words, not 2,000. If there is no written agreement about extra expenses, then the client could say that the fee includes all expenses. The contract should spell out any up-front money to be paid as well as the total fee.

The time frame should also be included. If the work is to be completed in sections, list the dates on which each part has to be done. For example, you may need to submit the first draft on April 15 and the final on June 30. Although it isn't required, I usually offer one free rewrite.

The contract should also describe what materials the client may provide, like leads, contacts, data, or records. Sometimes you need to include protection clauses that both parties agree to beforehand, to avoid misunderstandings in the future.

It's not that people are out to rip you off — the problem is that people often forget the details of agreements they've made over the telephone or in person. You probably forget occasionally too.

4. Invoices

I am baffled by the attitude among many writers that invoices are somehow tacky or even unprofessional. You've agreed to do a job and when it is done, you should bill the client, whether he or she is an editor, a corporate vice president, or a ghostwriting client.

Some writers advise billing the accounting department directly and skipping the editor's in-basket whenever possible. Some clients expect invoices and will give you a purchase order number to place on your invoice. This is good, because that means that accounting has already budgeted for your work and is planning to pay you. Sometimes you will receive two purchase order numbers: one for the main job and one for expenses.

Invoice forms are readily available in office supply stores and you can also buy them by mail order. However, I recommend you buy an inexpensive computer invoice program so your invoice printouts look more professional (see Sample 14 for an invoice). These programs also provide you with a good way to track your payments. Many invoice programs allow you to look at a register of all your receivables. (Money owed to you is receivable. Money you owe is accounts payable.)

One caution: some invoice programs are far too complex for the number of invoices that most writers need to send out. Go for simple, rather than for lots of frills. (I create my own invoices in Word.)

Remember that when you invoice customers, most clients won't pay you for about 30 days because that is an industry standard. If you've negotiated to receive immediate payment, be sure to state this

Book publishing contracts usually give authors royalties on each copy sold, so you won't know how much you have earned until you receive your royalty statement. A check to cover royalties usually comes with the statement.

Sample Invoice

Wally Writer
4 Treehouse Court
Columbia, ME 00000

INVOICE 462
July 25, 20—

XYZ Corporation
59 Elm Street
Columbia, ME 00000

Terms: 30 days

Description	Amount
Article on tree pruning for October issue	$400
Expenses (see attached annotated list)	57
Subtotal	457
Total	$457
Amount paid	$0
Amount due	$457

Annotated Telephone Expense List for XYZ Corporation Job, submitted July 25, 20-

Date	Called	Telephone Number	Charge
6/13/20-	Reba MacIntosh Treeworld	(312)464-5555	$7.97
6/15	Arthur Gala Gala Gardens	(303)987-5555	3.00
6/16	Lisa Golden Silver Threads	(860)431-5555	2.03
6/16	Tom Tangerine Manfred Company	(941)532-5555	6.47
6/16	Lacey Rome Jules Ianni, Inc.	(503)999-5555	5.00
6/17	Grace Smith Jefferson Foods	(212)567-5555	5.53
6/17	Elaine Valencia Happy Manors Ltd.	(727)549-5555	8.97
6/17	Prunella Peach Fruitaholics Inc.	(305)981-5555	13.03
6/17	Professor Plum Not a Clue	(603)908-5555	5.00

on the invoice itself. You still may not get paid for 30 days! At which time, you give the client another chance, by rebilling and putting SECOND NOTICE in large letters on the top of the bill.

4.1 What if you don't get paid?

Sometimes that awful thing happens — money that is owed to you is not paid. The editor doesn't return your calls, the article has been published, and you're worried you're never going to see that check. You had a contract, you invoiced them, but still, no payment. Should you give up?

No! Editors are sometimes great with words and awful with money. They may forget to turn in your invoice to the accounting department, lose it, or just consider it a low priority.

The first thing you should do is call. If the editor won't speak to you, will the publisher? Contacting the publisher directly has worked for me. Some writers recommend you call the accounting department, after first having sent the invoice to the accounting department. (Sometimes the accounting department will pay the invoice right away, so you won't get to the having-to-call stage.)

You can write dunning letters too, but I advise holding off on those. Everyone hates threats, and that's your final piece of ammunition in the battle, so you don't want to use it right away.

Sometimes writers' groups will intercede for you. They have varying track records at recovery. Also, in some cases, writers' groups have contracted with actual collection agencies. A collection agency is not likely to be interested unless the fee is over several hundred dollars. (Collection agencies keep a percentage of the amount collected.)

It is also important to note that when a client owes you money that was due over 60 days ago, you should not do any more work for that client. This seems self-evident, yet many writers continue to write, essentially for free. This is not good practice. Holding off on providing any further copy may be just the incentive the company needs to release your money to you.

Are there times when you just won't get paid or shouldn't pursue payment? Yes, for example, when a client still owes you $25 and it would cost you three hours to collect it in letters, telephone calls, and so forth — and you still might not collect — it may not be worth pursuing. Sometimes it's worth it to write it off as a bad debt.

I think many writers give up far too easily, but there is a point where it is unreasonable to keep going. You will need to determine where that point is for you.

4.2 The last-ditch secret weapon for getting paid for magazine articles

Years ago I had trouble receiving payment for some magazine articles I had written and that were published. I had sent invoices, made calls, written letters, all to no avail. Then I went to a writer's conference and complained to a fellow writer and she told me about her secret tactic that always worked for her. I have only used it twice and it worked both times. No promises however!

Here's the deal. If it's more than 60 to 90 days after publication and there's been no sign of money and no indication of when or if you'll ever receive anything, consider trying this. Write a letter complaining about the editor and the publication to *Writer's Digest* magazine (or another national writers publication. Local or regional is not good enough). You explain the problem factually and concisely to the editor, whose name you will have looked up. You also can allude to all sorts of enclosures that you may (or may not) have.

Now it gets more complicated. You *advance date* the letter and DO NOT send it. Why? Because your main letter is the cover letter to the nonpaying customer. This states flatly and briefly that if you do not receive payment within the next five days (or some other brief period), then you will send the attached letter to *Writer's Digest*.

Send the letter to the bad customer, with your advance-dated complaint letter enclosed. And be ready to actually send the other letter if you receive no reply.

I've never had to send it. Within two to three days, I was paid in full.

Why did this work? Would the writers magazine have done anything? I have no idea. I never had to send the letter — although I would have, if payment had not arrived promptly. The thing is, the client recalcitrant about paying debts doesn't know what would happen either. But the risk of seeing his or her name, and the publication's name, in print in a negative light can be enough to shake loose some money.

This is a last-ditch attempt. After this, the only recourse you have is to sue the client in court, perhaps in a small claims court. Keep in mind that you won't be on friendly terms with this client after you send your threatening letter. But then, do you really want to be nice to deadbeats who use your work and never pay you? I would not.

5. Basic planning you should do

You don't have to become an accountant or financial genius to do some basic managing of your freelance finances. But you should keep track of earnings, as discussed in the next chapter on record-keeping, and you should also do some basic financial projections, including a cash flow projection and earnings projection, described in chapter 14. If you missed that part, go back!

CHAPTER 16

Record-Keeping

Although you may not enjoy it, as a businessperson you need to keep and maintain orderly records. Keep track of your expenses, including telephone, stationery, printing, and photocopies, as well as large expenditures for equipment. You'll need this information for tax deductions and depreciation expenses, and to figure out if you are making a profit.

1. What to keep track of

1.1 Telephone and fax expenses

Although some writers scoff at tracking telephone calls, I think it is very important to note all long distance calls, including who was called or faxed, when, and the telephone or fax number. When you get your telephone bill, write in how much each call cost. Sample 15 shows the format of a telephone log I use to track calls. Keep your telephone log in a stand-alone book or notebook.

There are several advantages to tracking calls. First, as mentioned in past chapters, if you are being reimbursed for your telephone expenses, then you can verify that you made the calls.

Telephone Log

Date Called	Telephone Number	Charge	Client	Interviewee
5/23	(555) 555-3333	$2.49	Joan Brown, Marketing	Raj Singh
5/23	(555) 555-9876	$7.87	Mark Heart Press, ABC	Tony Espinoza
5/24	(904) 555-3333	$48.00	Dr. Jones, University of Florida	Andy Fred

Often you may need to call former interviewees back, either to clarify something they said or to use them as sources for future articles, books, or projects. If you can look up the telephone number in your log, you save valuable time. You should also maintain a Rolodex (electronic or manual) of important contacts.

In addition, once you get used to tracking your calls, you will consciously and unconsciously develop a feel for what is a reasonable amount of time for a telephone call, depending on the subject, who your client is, and how much he or she pays. As a result, you will be more practical and more efficient; you may realize that it might be good for you to call some interviewees after 5:00 p.m., especially if you are on the east coast and they are on the west coast, in order to take advantage of lower rates.

Even when the client covers your expenses, when you run up expensive telephone bills, it is you who has to front the costs. When you get your bill, submit an invoice. Thirty days later you may be paid. You lose the use of that money for over a month, affecting your cash flow.

Also, your client doesn't pay you any interest, just the exact amount charged. Consequently, it is cost-effective for you to be frugal whenever possible, even when expenses are to be reimbursed. Keeping track of telephone bills helps you trim expenses.

Some writers believe it is all right to offer an estimate of expenses and not bother to keep track. The problem is that you end up undercharging your customer.

It is true that recording and later tracking telephone calls takes time. However, it takes only a few minutes to record your calls for the day. You can jot them down after each call or at the end of the day. This is much easier than trying to reconstruct your record of calls a month later when the bill arrives.

Include the name of the client with your telephone log. This is useful if you are working for several clients at the same time. I generally write down the first name of the editor and that works for me. You may want to write down first and last names and/or the name of the publication.

1.2 Other expenses

An entrepreneurial writer incurs many overhead expenses that clients cannot cover: paper, postage, diskettes, and other items. Maintain a listing of these expenses for your own purposes (as well as for tax purposes) so you know how profitable you are and what areas you need to become more efficient in.

For example, if you find your paper expenses are high, determine why. Is it because you print out every single draft that you've written? Would it be more cost-effective and efficient, in such a case, to compose directly on the computer and print out only a final draft, if that? Or are you buying small packages of paper every week or every month instead of buying one bulk package of paper every six months? Bulk purchases often end up being cheaper.

The more aware you are of your spending patterns, the better you can control them. Businesses are always looking for ways to cut expenses, and you, as a businessperson, should also make attempts to improve your bottom line through cutting costs.

1.3 Record your earnings

Make sure that you record a check the day it arrives. You may think the check amount is emblazoned on your brain — but you can forget. So write it down. Many people keep a record of revenues in the same place they record expenses. If you have an invoice program, you can input the payment when it is received.

Record when the check was received, who it was from, the amount, and the name of the publication or company.

Try to record payments (and expenses) the day they happen. You think you'll never ever forget a check for $2,000 or more, and you may not. However, you may later ask yourself when it came in. Was it June or July? Was it 2001 or 2002? Keep a record and you'll know for sure.

1.4 A personal journal

You may wish to keep a personal journal where you record goals and achievements as well as what you hope to accomplish over the next few months. It can be informal and written in longhand or it could be typed and saved in a computer file. If you do keep such a journal, consider it as another record-keeping device, one that can help you keep on track and be more organized. A journal is also a good place to write down ideas and generate creativity.

2. Taxes

Although taxation is a topic that makes most people groan, it is important to keep in mind that a profit-making writer will need to pay income tax.

It is impossible to cover all or even a small part of the tax issues involved in running a home business. The point is that without adequate records, you will be unable to assess what taxes you owe, and nor will anybody else. You certainly do not want to overpay.

In some cases, your clients can provide you with that information. In the United States, most clients send writers annual statements that show how much was paid in the previous year. These forms are also sent to the Internal Revenue Service. Always check with your government tax office for the latest requirements. For more information on dealing with the Internal Revenue Service, look at *Tax This! An Insider's Guide to Standing Up to the IRS,* another title in the Self-Counsel Series.

In Canada, contact Revenue Canada for more information on the records you need to keep and the deductions you are eligible for. You will also need to decide if you are going to charge GST.

3. Paper records

3.1 Project research and records

Although not required by tax authorities or your clients, I think it is a good idea to retain the research material for a project for at least a year or so. You can go back and use it again if you need to, or you can answer any questions that may come up after your work is published.

Choose an appropriate file folder for the size of the project and label it. For voluminous projects, you may want to use heavy accordion-style folders or even boxes. For smaller projects, use file folders. When you come up with a way to spin off an old idea, you can pull out that folder and reuse and update the material.

3.2 Business correspondence

It is also important to maintain several correspondence files. If you're a heavy communicator, you may want to make monthly or semi-annual folders. If you don't write or receive a lot of letters, then you could make an annual file. Be sure to print out and save business e-mails from editors and other clients.

I recommend you create a file for "Letters Received" and a separate file for "Letters Sent." Or you can organize your files by project and attach the letters you send with the responses.

It is a good idea to have a separate file for contracts. Although you may not refer to this file very often, it will be easy to find when you need it. You can put the contracts in alphabetical order or some other order — you're in charge so make your own plan.

Whatever system you use, create one that works for you and change it when it no longer works. You will know how well it works by how hard it is to find things. If it takes you an hour to find a contract or a letter you wrote last month, your system needs to be rethought.

3.3 Your clips

It is also a good idea to create a file of published clips. When you find a new client, invariably he or wants to see samples of your past work. If you have many clips, you can separate these into files of business articles, social science articles, etc. Or you can be more specific and separate them into articles on "Total quality management," "Egyptian hieroglyphics," and so on.

Incidentally, don't send your prospective clients originals of your clips if you can avoid it. Send photocopies and preserve the originals. Only send out originals if you have plenty of extra ones.

CHAPTER 17

Have a Life!

When you're working on a particularly fascinating article or project, it is easy to lose track of time and forget the basics like sleeping and eating.

Don't chain yourself to your computer. You'll hurt your back, and I suspect your mind may atrophy as well.

When you become very involved with a project, you can also become obsessed, which is okay in the short term. However, don't forget to enjoy your life. A good writer is also a well-rounded person. Get some exercise, go for a walk, or go to the gym. Take your kids for a trip. Visit another city and gain a new perspective. Live!

Although there will be days when you really must work long hours in order to get a project done, this should not be a way of life, day-in, day-out. You could rapidly become burned out.

One major drawback of working at home is the danger of becoming obsessed with working too hard.

If the only way to tear yourself away from work is to actually schedule time alone or with your spouse or kids, then do so. Remember that staff employees are given periodic breaks and time off for lunch, and you should be at least as kind to yourself.

In this book I hope I've forewarned you sufficiently so you can avoid many mistakes and problems. Freelance writing can be rewarding, but keep in mind that it is a business.

I hope you find your writing business intriguing and profitable. Today is the information age. More than ever, people need clear, concise, accurate, well-written information. This need can only accelerate; as a writer, you can be an important and integral part of this very exciting era.

Appendix

1. Important books for writers

Writer's Guide to Book Editors, Publishers, and Literary Agents

Jeff Herman
Prima Publishing
3000 Lava Ridge Court
Roseville, CA 95661

This book is a must for those interested in book publishing. Lists book editors and agents and their interests.

The Writer's Market

Writer's Digest Books
1507 Dana Avenue
Cincinnati, OH 45207

An annual guide that includes thousands of listings of popular and trade buyers, including book publishers, magazines, script buyers, syndicates, and greeting card publishers.

Writing for the Web
Crawford Kilian
Self-Counsel Press
1481 Charlotte Road
North Vancouver, BC V7J 1H1

A comprehensive guide to writing copy for the Internet and Intranets.

2. Magazines and newsletters

2.1 United States

Freelance Success

801 NE 70th Street
Miami, FL 33138
Tel: (305) 757-8854
Web site: www.freelancesuccess.com

A marketing and management guide for professional writers.

Freelance Writer's Report

Cassell Communications
P.O. Box A
North Stratford, NH 03590
Tel: (800) 351-9278 (toll free in United States and Canada)
Web site: www.writers-editors.com

Monthly newsletter with market listings and practical advice.

Publishers Weekly

249 W. 17th Street
New York, NY 10011
Web site: www.publishersweekly.com

Weekly, concentrates on book industry.

The Writer

120 Boylston Street
Boston, MA 02116-4615
Tel: (617) 423-4615

For new fiction writers.

Writer's Digest

1507 Dana Avenue
Cincinnati, OH 45207
Tel: (513) 531-2222
Web site: www.writersdigest.com

Published monthly; heavy on helpful how-to information for beginners.

Writer's Journal

P.O. Box 394
Perham, MN 56573-0394
Tel: (218) 346-7921
Web site: www.sowashco.com/writersjournal

Heavy on how-to for both nonfiction and fiction writers.

2.2 Canada

Canadian Writer's Journal

Box 5180
New Liskeard, ON P0J 1P0
Web site: www.nt.net/~cwj/index.htm

Quarterly magazine.

3. Organizations for writers

3.1 United States

Note: Canadians may also wish to check out and possibly join some of the following organizations.

American Medical Writers Association

40 West Guide Drive, Suite 101
Rockville, MD 20850-1192
Tel: (301) 294-5303
Web site: www.amwa.org

For writers specializing in medical topics.

American Society of Journalists & Authors

Suite 302, 1501 Broadway
New York, NY 10036
Tel: (212) 997-0947
Web site: www.asja.org

For experienced writers and authors.

Association of Authors' Representatives, Inc.

P.O. Box 237201, Ansonia Station
New York, NY 10003
Web site: www.bookwire.com/AAR

Information on literary agents who are members.

The Authors Guild

330 W. 42nd Street, 29th Floor
New York, NY 10036
Tel: (212) 563-5904
Web site: www.authorsguild.org

For published authors.

National Association of Science Writers

P.O. Box 294
Greenlawn, NY 11740
Tel: (516) 757-5664
Web site: www.nasw.org/

Freelancers and employees of major newspapers and periodicals.

National Writers Association

3140 S. Peoria Street, 295PMB
Aurora, CO 80014
Tel: (303) 841-0246
Web site: www.nationalwriters.com

Screenwriters, novelists, poets, freelance writers.

Society of Children's Book Writers and Illustrators

8271 Beverly Boulevard
Los Angeles, CA 90048
Tel: (323) 782-1010
Web site: www.scbwi.org/

> For professionals and beginners.

Society for Technical Communication

901 N. Stuart Street, Suite 904
Arlington, VA 22203-1822
Tel: (703) 522-4114
Web site: www.stc.org

> For technical writers.

Writers Guild of America, West

7000 West Third St
Los Angeles, CA 90048
Tel: (800) 548-4532
Web site: www.wga.org/

> For screenwriters and scriptwriters

3.2 Canada

Canadian Association of Journalists

Carleton University, St. Patrick's Building
1125 Colonel By Drive
Ottawa, ON K1S 5B6
Tel: (613) 526-8061
Web site: www.eagle.ca/caj/

Canadian Authors Association

Box 419
Campbellford, ON K0L 1L0
Tel: (705) 653-0323
Web site: www.islandnet.com/~caa/national.html

Canadian Society of Children's Authors, Illustrators, and Performers (CANSCAIP)

35 Spadina Rd.
Toronto, ON M5R 2S9
Tel: (416) 515-1559
Web site: www.interlog.com/~canscaip/

Professionals in the field of children's culture.

Editors' Association of Canada
35 Spadina Road
Toronto, ON M5R 2S9
Tel: (416) 975-1379
Web site: www.editors.ca

Federation of British Columbia Writers

600-890 West Pender Street
Vancouver, BC V6C 1K4
Tel: (604) 683-2057
Web site: www.swifty.com/bcwa/index.html

Purportedly the largest writers organization in British Columbia.

Periodical Writers Association of Canada (PWAC)

54 Wolseley Street, Suite 203
Toronto, ON M5T 1A5
Tel: (416) 504-1645
Web site: www.pwac.ca

Writers' Federation of Nova Scotia
1113 Marginal Road
Halifax, NS B3H 4P7
Tel: (902) 423-8116
Web site: www.chebucto.ns.ca/Culture/WritersFed/

Writers' Union of Canada

24 Ryerson Avenue
Toronto, ON M5T 2P3
Tel: (416) 703-8982
Web site: www.swifty.com/twuc/index.htm

Members are Canadian authors.

Writers' Union of Canada (Vancouver office)

3102 Main Street, 3rd Floor
Vancouver, BC V4A 3C7
Tel/fax: (604) 874-1611
Web site: www.swifty.com/twuc/pacific.htm

4. Web sites with jobs for writers

Note: I didn't separate US and Canadian sites into two lists here because I think these lists may be potentially useful to both Americans and Canadians.

Authorlink
www.authorlink.com/jobavail.html

Freelance Writers Markets Pages
freelancewrite.miningco.com/business/freelancewrite/index.htm

(Note: I didn't forget the "www." You don't need it for the above address.)

Jeff Gaulin's Journalism Job Board (for Canadian writers)
www.direct.ca/continence/jobs/message.htm

Inkspot Writers' Classifieds Markets
www.inkspot.com/classifieds/mkt.html

Inkspot Writers' Classifieds: Jobs for Writers
www.inkspot.com/classifieds/writingjobs.html

Sunoasis Jobs
www.sunoasis.com/freelance.html

5. Online (listserv) newsletters for writers

The following are Web site or e-mail addresses for free newsletters that you can have sent to your e-mail address upon request.

Canadian Freelance News
www.proofpositive.com

Inklings
www.inkspot.com

Glossary

Advance: An amount an author receives against royalties. Not all publishers pay advances. If an author receives, for example, a $5,000 advance, this amount is deducted from later earnings of the book and is reported on the royalty statement. Therefore, if the book earns back $5,100 in royalties accrued over a six-month period (based on the royalty percentage the author and publisher have agreed upon), then the author will receive a check for $100.

Clips or clippings: Pieces that you have already written and had published. Although some writers send manuscript sheets to potential customers or markets, many photocopy previously published pieces and send them along with a query letter.

Contract: A written or verbal agreement between writer and publisher (or editor, businessperson, individual) to do work. Whenever possible, get it in writing. There is too much room for confusion otherwise.

Deadline: This is the date when the article, book, or project is due. Although some editors give an earlier-than-needed deadline to the writer, many tell the writer exactly when the piece is needed. If space is saved for a writer's piece and it doesn't arrive on time, it creates extra work for an editor and a time crunch. He or she won't hire you again unless you have a very good reason for being late. Tell an editor up front if you're running into a problem or can't complete a job on time so that he or she can suggest a solution or make other plans.

Expenses: Writers should always ask magazine editors and other contacts if they will be reimbursed for expenses. (Book authors are usually not reimbursed, although some writers do make such arrangements.) Many editors will reimburse expenses for telephone, express mail, fax, interview, and travel outside your local area. Telephone expenses are based on actual costs and travel expenses vary with the client. Some editors will reimburse for overnight expenses and some will even give you their Federal Express number for shipping you have to do for the project.

First draft: This is the first complete version of your article, book, or other writing project. It implies that you are willing to make changes that your customer requests.

Graf or 'graph: Paragraph.

Invoice: A bill to the editor or publisher, listing the fee for the work and any reimbursable expenses. Some writers are horrified at the thought of submitting an invoice. Most editors and other customers consider invoices to be quite routine. In some cases, editors can give writers a purchase order number, which must be placed on the invoice. This means they have budgeted ahead for your article, which is good!

Generally, invoices are paid within about 30 days. State 30 days as your term of payment unless you have an agreement to be paid immediately. Note: Be sure to include your name and address on the invoice so the customer will know who to pay. Also, provide a few words or a sentence describing the project.

Kill fee: This is the amount an editor or publisher agrees ahead of time to pay the writer if the piece is not published. Usually it is a percentage of whatever amount would have been paid had the article been published, for example, 20% or 30%.

Manuscript or MS.: This refers to your written material, whether it's a printout, on a computer disk, or in a file that you e-mailed to the editor.

Market: Refers to where you plan to sell the piece. Your market may be travel magazines or health periodicals or retirement publications, depending on who you see as your ultimate readers. The word "market" is also used in book publishing to refer to those people you anticipate will buy the book you plan to write.

On speculation (on spec): This means you agree to write a piece that the editor may or may not publish, depending on whether he or she likes it or not. New writers often accept such terms to penetrate difficult markets.

Payment on acceptance: This means you will receive your money when the editor formally accepts the piece, which may coincide with when the piece is published, but usually means you are paid sooner. Clarify with each editor what he or she means by this term.

Payment on publication: One might think that the day your article is published is the day your check is sent out. In the real world, it may well mean 30 or even 60 days later.

Payment per word: Many editors pay authors by word count. Thus, if they pay $1 per word and want 1,000 words, they will pay $1,000. Note that this is usually per edited word, to avoid writers padding their copy to up the ante.

Query letter or query: This is a letter describing an article or book you would like to write. Queries for articles should be no more than one page, single-spaced.

Reverse contract: When your client refuses to create a contract and you want to do the job anyway, create a reverse contract. Write a summation of what you think the client wants and send it to him or her. Ask the client to initial it and send it back to you.

Rights: This refers to what you have agreed to sell to your customer. If your customer buys "all rights," then that means you can't sell the piece to anyone else. If he or she buys "first rights," then you may sell the piece as a "reprint" to another customer, usually a noncompeting publication. Many writers sell the same piece over and over to different markets, while others use the same research to reslant and rewrite the article.

Royalty: A term used in book publishing that refers to the percentage of the receipts earned on book sales that the author will receive. Royalties may be based on the selling price of a book, on net sales, or on many other variables. Royalty statements are usually provided to authors semi-annually.

SASE: Self-addressed stamped envelope. Many magazine editors and publishers request that you enclose a SASE with your query or book proposal.

Slant: This refers to the key thread underlying your article or written piece. For example, for an article about parenting, your basic subject may be how parents over 40 with new babies differ from parents in their 20s. Your slant may be on the psychological effects of kids on older parents versus younger parents. It could be on the health of older parents versus younger parents, or on how children who are now grown up viewed their parents at these ages.

The slant of an article or piece is very important because it determines what research you use. It encompasses viewpoint as well. You may presume ahead of time that older parents are "better" or "worse" and your editor may ask you to find supporting evidence.

Word count: Most editors know approximately how long they want a written piece to be. It could be 500 words, 1,000 words, 2,000 words, or more. Usually, the length is expressed in hundreds or thousands of words. A double-spaced page of copy contains about 250 words. Many computer programs can calculate a word count for you. The editor may edit your work down from what was requested.

It is important to note that newspaper editors often use the term "column inch," which refers to the number of words in an inch of column space. If you want to know how many words that is, find a copy of the publication and measure it off in one-inch squares, then count the number of words in that block. The number of words in a column inch varies from publication to publication because they use different type fonts and styles.

OTHER TITLES IN THE SELF-COUNSEL WRITING SERIES

Writing Horror

Edo van Belkom

$19.95

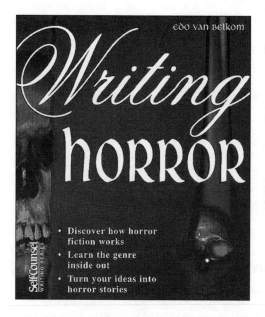

- Discover how horror fiction works

- Learn the genre inside out

- Turn your ideas into horror stories

Think you have the makings of a goor horror writer? The craft of horror fiction has its own rules. *Writing Horror* takes you through the process of creating horror, including the art of suspending reader disbelief, the creation of atmosphere and believable characters, and the seven steps of plotting. From psychological to supernatural horror, from vampires to splatterpunk, *Writing Horror* gives you practical advice on starting and finishing your manuscript, getting a response from publishers, and cracking the pro market.

Writing Travel Books and Articles

Richard Cropp, Barbara Braidwood, and Susan M. Boyce

$15.95

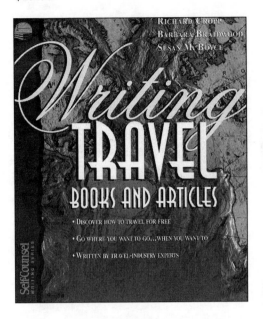

- Discover how to travel for free

- Go where you want to go...when you want to go

- Learn from travel-industry experts

Do you love to travel to exotic and exciting destinations? Is writing your passion? Imagine being paid to do both as a travel writer! Offering guaranteed job satisfaction, travel writing has many fringe benefits such as getting behind-the-scenes information and traveling to your favorite destinations.

Written by experienced travel writers, this guide will show you how to get those all-important free trips and get your travel writing published. Ideal for the novice writer, and full of helpful tips for the experienced travel writer, this information-packed book includes finding sponsors, getting your first article published, publishing on the Internet, and common mistakes of new travel writers.

Writing for the Web

Crawford Kilian

$15.95

- Hook surfers' attention

- Write informative, persuasive Web text

- Create dynamic personal and corporate Web pages

Hundreds of books have appeared recently on how to design new Web pages and jazz up existing Web sites with graphics, sounds, and links. But effective Web sites contain much more than far-out videos, graphics, and sounds – they also contain text that people will want to read. Writing for the Web demands a different kind of writing, one that incorporates the styles of both print and TV writing.

Writing for the Web offers sound principles that writers should bear in mind as well as exercises to strengthen writing skills and eliminate bad writing habits. The principles are based on the author's firsthand experience and on the experience of organizations that rely on Web communications for their very existence.

Order Form

All prices are subject to change without notice. Books are available in book, department, and stationery stores. If you cannot buy the book through a store, please use this order form. (Please print.)

Name _____

Address _____

Charge to: ☐ Visa   ☐ MasterCard

Account number _____

Validation date_____

Expiry date_____

Signature _____

YES, please send me:

_____ Writing Horror; $19.95

_____ Writing Travel Books and Articles; $15.95

_____ Writing for the Web; $15.95

Please add $3.00 for postage and handling.

Canadian residents, please add 7% GST to your order.

WA residents, please add 7.8% sales tax.

☐ Check here for a free catalogue.

IN CANADA
Please send your order to the nearest location:

Self-Counsel Press   Self-Counsel Press
1481 Charlotte Road   4 Bram Court
North Vancouver, BC V7J 1H1   Brampton, ON L6W 3R6

IN THE U.S.A.
Please send your order to:

Self-Counsel Press Inc.
1704 N. State Street
Bellingham, WA 98225

Visit our Web site at: *www.self-counsel.com*